Crossing the Goal Line...
Ten Yards at a Time

Crossing the Goal Line...
Ten Yards at a Time

Marcus Hester

Family Life International
Chicago, Illinois

Crossing the Goal Line...Ten Yards at a Time
Published by:
Hester International Publications
P.O. Box 9121
Winnetka, IL 60093 USA
(847) 267-9430
ISBN 0-9669086-0-0

Editorial Consultants: Steve Johnston and Debbie McCormick

Cover design and book production by:
DB & Associates Design & Distribution
dba Double Blessing Productions
P.O. Box 52756, Tulsa, OK 74152
www.dbassoc.org

Printed in the United States of America.

Dedication

To my wife Sharon, daughter Ashly, and son Joshua, who loved me through the entire process of writing this book. *I love you...*thank you for your sacrifice and patience.

Contents

Foreword

When dealing with a subject as intense as warfare, we must realize that it is not those that sit in the dusty, lofty halls in the citadels of education that are the experts; but instead it is those that have smelled the smoke and grease from the guns, and understand the true commitment and principles which are needed for successful engagement.

Marcus Hester speaks to us from the trenches of Chicago with clear definition direction, that any Christian could use to take him into battle against principalities and powers. Christians are prone to call prayer "Spiritual warfare" but really war at every level is spiritual. Even the current conflicts in the world today are the results of a spiritual conflict.

Throughout Christianity there are the voices that cry out for balance, but no war can ever be fought balanced. It is only those that live in the extreme that will ever smell the sweet flowers of success, which grow long after victory has been secured. When many refer to balance they are really advising us to engagement. Biblical history and secular history have taught us the stupidity of such a stand. The countries of Poland, Austria, and France; just to name a few, were seduced by the wonderful peace declarations of Adolph Hitler. Not realizing that at the same moment he was amassing the greatest technical army, "Blitzkrieg" that the world had ever seen.

This was the pathway that the enemy chose for victory; no wonder France fell in a few days. Don't forget, England tried to conquer France and that war lasted for one hundred years without complete success.

This book is calling for all out war against the powers of darkness in our nation. This will require a new commitment to prayer, fasting, witnessing, and even reorganizing your church.

Thank you Marcus Hester for reminding us the importance of the daunting task before us.

—Richard Gazowsky
Christian WYSIWYG
Filmworks, Inc.
San Francisco, CA

Introduction

Finish the Job

Jesus saith unto them, My meat is to do the will of him that sent me, and to finish his work.

John 4:34

The all important question is not how you *started* a mission, but how you *finished* the mission. One is rarely remembered for how one started in life, but what was accomplished when it is all over. When we think of the famous public speaker Zig Zigler, we do not remember the 2,000 speeches he made without receiving one single dime, but we knew this world renowned man for his motivational speeches that brought thousands to hear him at over $100 per ticket. We have all heard of Walt Disney World in Orlando, Florida. We gaze upon the grand theme park that attracts tourists from around the world, rarely knowing that Walt Disney declared bankruptcy three times before he made a success of Disneyland. We have all heard of Popeye's Chicken from New Orleans, a chicken franchise that is known around the world. How did this restaurant start? Many do not know. Al Copeland came from the projects in New Orleans and did not finish high school. He started a donut shop that went out of business. He then started a small chicken stand, and the rest is history. In sports, they say, winning is everything…well, in God's team…

finishing is everything. Be sure to read our *second book,* called, *Finishing The Job: A New Look at an Old Command.* This book will bring clarity to the *"job"* we must finish as Believers. But before we can start a race, we must first be *prepared.* Before we step up to the starting line, our *character* must be developed. Before we can be faithful in much, we must be *faithful in a little.* Before we can bring order to the house of God, we must bring order to our own house (personal lives).

(For if a man know not how to *rule his own house,* how shall he take care of the church of God?)

1 Timothy 3:5

When I was meditating on what God wanted to speak through this book to His sons and daughters, the Lord put on my heart that this book was to be of help for *three different* groups of believers. This book can help **prepare** the Christians who have a "calling" on their lives whether they are (1) in the wilderness, (2) actually in "the call" and pursuing God's vision, or (3) approaching the end of their mission in life. I hope this book will help *expose* the devil's schemes used against the Body of Christ as he tries to *slow them down* from fulfilling God's plan for their life. I hope this book will be used by men and women of God to *HELP PREPARE* them for the *LONG HAUL* as they fulfill God's destiny. I hope this book will help our church leaders *"FINISH THE JOB"* that God has commissioned them to do. **LET US ALL CROSS THE GOAL LINE TOGETHER…TEN YARDS AT A TIME** with Jesus Christ as the author and finisher of our faith.

Run The Race To Win

Know ye not that they which run in a race run all, but one receiveth the prize? *So run, that ye may obtain* [win].

And every man that striveth for the mastery is temperate in all things. Now they do it to obtain a corruptible crown; but we an incorruptible.

I therefore so run, not as uncertainly; so fight I, not as one that beateth the air:

But I keep under my body, and bring it into subjection: lest that by any means, *when I have preached to others, I myself should be a castaway.*
1 Corinthians 9:24-27

As a minister's son, I saw many young men go to seminary who I knew should *not* have been there...who were not "*called*" by God. I knew that it was only a matter of time before they would drop out and quit. The Lord says that, "many are called, but *few are chosen*" (Matthew 22:14). The ones that God "calls" are the *only* ones that Satan is worried about. Satan knows that the ones "*sent*" by God are the ones anointed and empowered, who can hurt his kingdom.

In this book, we have identified *TEN SPIRITUAL WEAPONS* that Satan will use against you at sometime in your life if you are "called" of God. We have identified *TEN HURDLES* that you must jump over before you walk into the "fullness" of your calling. We have identified *TEN CHARACTER BUILDER TESTS* that God has designed for you to walk victoriously through before you accomplish God's plan for your life. For example, in one of the chapters, we discuss the "Spirit of Division." One of the major weapons Satan uses to divide ministries, marriages, and the Body of Christ is "offense." Will you ever be offended on this earth? *You bet you will!* Satan will use someone to offend you (either Christian or non-Christian). How will you respond? Your response can determine your destiny in this life. The Bible says that offense will come. The question is not if it will come, but when it comes, *how will you respond*? Are you going to walk in love, or are you going to react in the flesh? Satan has used this *simple weapon of offense* as a major tool to divide his people for thousands of years. Let us wake up! Satan does not need new weapons, the old ones still work just fine. RUN THE RACE TO WIN, and *if you know in advance* what some of the tactics Satan will throw at you are, then you will be ready for them, not falling under Satan's traps and keeping you from your victory.

Slowed Down, Diverted, and Stopped

Satan's **TOP TEN HIT LIST** of weapons will be used against you and he will use "some or all" of them to either (1) slow you down, (2) divert you, or (3) stop you from walking in the *"perfect plan"* that God has called you to. If he succeeds in *any* one of these *three* areas, *he will be successful*. Let us not give the devil an inch. Let us hold our ground. Let us keep our eyes on Jesus, not being slowed down, diverted, or stopped by Satan. Let us run the race with our destiny in mind. Let us run the race with a purpose. Let us run the race informed. *Let us run the race to win!*

According to Webster's Dictionary, a *castaway* is a person that has been shipwrecked. Let us not be a shipwrecked Christian. Let us not be another casualty of war, but a Christian with his rudder pointed straight towards Jesus, steady in the will of God. God's leaders and the group of Christians God has entrusted you to oversee are important, but God has proper order and priorities that must be "set in place" to have a *balanced* ministry. If you love your church more than your wife and family, you are not in God's proper order. If you preach on holiness and you are walking in sin, you are out of God's order. If you are a church leader, let me say it like this, "God is more concerned about you (your character) than your ministry." God is interested in giving you His anointing, but He is *more interested* in *first* developing your character.

For example, Samson had the strength and the anointing of God, but he was defeated (not finishing the race), because his character was out of order. *It says to be not ignorant of Satan's schemes* (2 Corinthians 2:11). In this book, we are going to shed the light of God and dispel the darkness of Satan's camp. As the Body of Christ, it is time we wake up to the schemes of the devil. It is time to tell the devil, *ENOUGH IS ENOUGH!* I hope after you read this book, you will say, "I am now wise to you devil and you will not use these ten weapons against me any more because *no weapon* formed against me shall prosper."

> *No weapon that is formed against thee shall prosper;* and every tongue that shall rise against thee in judgment thou shalt condemn. This is the heritage of the servants of the LORD, and their righteousness is of me, saith the LORD.
>
> **Isaiah 54:17**

We are not here to glorify Satan, by talking about him, but we are here to *"expose and destroy the works of the devil"* (1 John 3:8). The word *expose* means, *"to make known the crime"* (Webster). Satan has *no legal ground* to attack you because Jesus defeated him on the cross. Satan is working against you *illegally*. Satan is an outlaw. Jesus says we are redeemed from the curse of the law (Galatians 3:13). So why does Satan still have victory over so many of God's people? *The promises of the Word are not automatic.* You must have (1) knowledge of them, (2) believe them and (3) continually fight for them. It is a crime to let someone steal from you. A criminal has no right to break into your home and rob you. If that happened, you would call 911 (police). In the same way, God's people are being robbed by the devil. He is stealing the blessings that are rightfully yours.

> **The thief cometh not, but for to *steal, and to kill, and to destroy:* I am come that they might have life, and that they might have it more abundantly.**
>
> **John 10:10**

First, we have to know what Satan is doing and what he is attacking us with. Secondly, when we know, *we can then fight back*. We must take back the ground that Satan has stolen. Our attitudes should be, "enough is enough, devil" It is time to rouse ourselves to war.

> **Proclaim this among the nations: *Prepare a war; rouse the mighty men!* Let all the soldiers draw near, let them come up!**
>
> **Joel 3:9 (NASB)**

My prayer is that this book will "stir" up your spirit to begin preparing for war, but even more, that you will become one of God's mighty warriors, not being slowed down, diverted, or stopped from fulfilling God's plan for your life.

Don't Strike The Rock

> **And Moses lifted up his hand, and with his rod *he smote the rock twice:* and the water came out abundantly, and the congregation drank, and their beasts also.**
>
> **And the LORD spake unto Moses and Aaron, Because ye believed me not, to sanctify me in the eyes of the children of Israel, *therefore ye shall not bring this congregation into the land which I have given them.***
>
> **Numbers 20:11,12**

One of the most tragic stories in the Bible is the story where Moses was never allowed to enter the Promised Land, because he "smote the rock" versus "speaking to the rock." Why did the action of Moses make the Lord so angry? Simply, Moses let the people frustrate him. Moses dishonored God in front of His people. Moses failed to show the true character of God. Are you ready to lead a group of people? Are you mature in character to properly portray the character of God? Moses had 40 years to prepare, and he failed the test. He failed to enter the promised land. *How tragic!* Thank God for the blood of Jesus. Thank God for His grace for us today. Moses spent 40 years in the wilderness. Moses spent another 40 years in the wilderness with the *complaining* Jewish people. And after only one mistake, he could not go into the promised land. You will be remembered not for how you start, but how you finish, either for good or bad. If you are a young minister longing to start your own church or lead a congregation, consider this…Moses spent 40 years in preparation and 40 years with the Israelites, and still failed to reach his promised land. Are you really ready? Is your character lined up like the character of Jesus? Are you not only prepared to start, but also finish the mission that God has called you to? Are you ready to *Cross the Goal Line…Ten Yards at a Time?*

The Goal Line

The title of this book is called, *Crossing the Goal Line …Ten Yards at a Time.* As an ex-football player, I learned a great many lessons that have helped me achieve success in life. Football taught me the lessons of success, such as hard work, discipline, goal setting, and teamwork to name a few. Still today, the sport of football has had a great deal to do with the character building of my life. I thank God for allowing me to be a part of this great American past time, from pee-wee football to college level football.

As I was thinking about all the heroes in the football arena, one man kept entering my mind. He is the famous Joe Montana, who was the quarterback for the San Francisco 49ers. Why was Joe Montana one of the best quarterbacks ever to play the game? He did not have the strongest throwing arm. He was not very fast on his feet. He was not physically tall or big. So why was he so successful? He was always *prepared* to play on game day.

His success on game day, was directly indicative of the amount of time and effort he gave in his practice sessions.

Joe Montana was not only prepared to play, but was also a *total player*. He knew how to play the *total game* of football. He rarely made big plays as quarterback, throwing the big bomb pass, but he was known for his control style of offense. He moved the ball down the field *Ten Yards at a Time*. With this "control style" of offense, he held on to the ball longer than his opponent, thus, wearing down his opponent. He controlled the game, thus his team *Crossed the Goal Line* more times than his opponent. Joe Montana and the San Francisco 49ers still have one of the most winning records in professional football.

Likewise, the Body of Christ and its leaders today, must be (1) *prepared*, (2) know the *total game*, and (3) *take control* of their lives. We must be prepared in our character development, we must know the entire Word of God, and we must take control of our destiny, not letting the devil steal our life from us.

God is not looking for just one big success, He is looking for faithfulness in obtaining victories in many *small successes*, *Ten Yards at a Time*. God wants you to have victory in your life, and *Cross the Goal Line...Ten Yards at a Time*.

A Son's Prayer

I was having lunch at a pastor's luncheon in Asheville, North Carolina. My father (a pastor as well) and I were at the Billy Graham Center in the beautiful mountains of the Blue Ridge Parkway. Each pastor in the group was praying for the ministries represented at the luncheon. Franklin Graham (Billy Graham's son) was praying for his father. Billy Graham, many know as a successful evangelist, but at that time he was entering the last leg of his ministry. Billy Graham is known for his integrity as a minister as he preached the Gospel around the world. Millions have accepted the Lord as a result of his crusades. Franklin Graham stood up and started praying, "Lord, help my dad finish the race. Lord help my dad obtain the prize. Lord help my dad *cross the goal line and not be disqualified.*" Tears came to my eyes as I heard Franklin pray. For right beside me was my own father, a pastor of 30 plus years himself. I prayed silently for my own dad. Likewise, Jesus, our heavenly Father, is praying for us to, *finish the race.* Jesus is cheering us on to, *Cross the Goal Line...Ten Yards at a Time.*

Being confident of this very thing, that he which hath *begun a good work in you will perform it* [finish it] *until the day of Jesus Christ.*

Philippians 1:6

Now, let us expose the "ten weapons" that Satan uses against the Saints to stop us from completing the work that the Lord has called us to. Let us not be slowed down, diverted, or stopped in our quest to *Cross the Goal Line.* Let us discover the "ten tools" of God that help us in our character development, thus preparing us for our ministry. Let us *Cross the Goal Line...Ten Yards at a Time.*

Crossing the Goal Line...
Ten Yards at a Time

Chapter 1

The Spirit of Deceit

Then the LORD God said to woman, "What is this you have done?" The woman said, "The serpent *deceived* me, and I ate."

Genesis 3:13 (NIV)

The reason I am writing about the *spirit of deceit first* is, because it was the *first trick* that Satan used against man. The woman said to God, "The serpent *deceived* me." It all started in the garden of Eden and Satan is still using the *"spirit of deceit"* today to trick God's children.

And he said, Take heed that ye *be not deceived:* for many shall come in my name, saying, I am Christ; and the time draweth near: go ye not therefore after them.

Luke 21:8

Satan's *two greatest weapons* that he uses against the Body of Christ are:

(1) being an accuser of the brethren and (2) deceiver of the brethren. According to Webster's dictionary, the word **deceive** means *"to make a person believe what is not true."* What a simple but very true definition. Satan does not have your best interest at heart but his own agenda in mind. The Greek word for *"deceive"* is *planao* which means to *"go astray or cause to roam from the truth."* Satan himself is even known as, *"the one who deceives."*

1

> **And the great dragon was cast out, that old serpent, called the Devil, and Satan, which *deceiveth the whole world:* he was cast out into the earth, and his angels were cast out with him.**
>
> **Revelation 12:9**

Satan is the master of deception. The *spirit of deceit* is a major weapon that Satan uses against God's people. This spirit can literally slow you down or stop you from fulfilling God's will for your life. Why is Satan so successful in using the *spirit of deceit* against us? Simply, we have not developed discernment for this *spirit of deceit* and we have not grasped a good working knowledge of the Word of God (Bible). In this chapter, let us look at some examples in the Word of how God's people responded "rightly or wrongly" to Satan's weapon, the *spirit of deceit*.

Natural World Versus Spiritual World

What does discernment mean? I am not talking about worldly discernment, perceiving things of the natural eye, but discernment, in the spiritual world. The *spiritual* world is just as real as the *natural* world. Just because you cannot see it with the naked eye does not mean it does not exist. *It is real.* In God's Word it says, *"we do not wrestle against flesh and blood, but against principalities"* (Ephesians 6:10). It is time that we recognize, that the natural victories we obtain on this earth were *first* won in the heavenlies (spiritual arena).

I want to make a quick statement of warning regarding the *spirit of deceit*. I am not advocating being "suspicious" of everyone and everything. God will send faithful people to work along side of you in ministry. We have to be able to trust people, *but not all people who come to assist you in the work of the Lord are from God; not every door that is open was opened by God.* We have to be able to

2

develop discernment of our natural world with our spiritual eyes. It is a *process* as God builds experience and wisdom into your life.

The Sovereignty of God

God is sovereign. He is supreme and independent of man. He has all authority. One major mistake within the Body of Christ is to just sit back and watch God work, playing *no part* in establishing God's kingdom on earth. We are a co-laborer with Christ. Sometimes, our attitude as Christians is, "whatever will be will be." Yes, God is sovereign, *but God has given **us the tools** to possess the land*. He has given us our cities, and our families, but we have to drive the devil out of our land, out of our marriages, out of our churches, out of our cities and out of our nations. If we do not do this, it will not be done. We are waiting on God, but God is waiting on us. He is waiting on us to take back what is rightfully ours. Do not be deceived by not *knowing or doing* God's will for your life. Once again, be sure to read the book, *How to Finish The Job: A New Look at an Old Command*. This book goes into greater detail describing the mission of every believer.

By Doing Nothing, We lose

We have to wake up to the fact that we are in a war! Not just a one time battle, but a daily battle. Are you taking up your cross daily? In our apathy, the Promised Land that God has given His Church (Body of Christ) is under siege by the devil. The Church is being deceived by doing nothing. We are waiting on God, but God is waiting on you. Satan is driving your new car that you have been hoping for. He is living in your new home. Satan has your new church property.

How can you fight in a war if you do not know you are in one? How can you win in a battle if you do not know your enemy? How can you even dare to win if you do not know your opponent's schemes and strategies?

> **lest Satan should take advantage of us; for we are
> *not ignorant of his devices.***
>
> **2 Corinthians 2:11 (NKJV)**

God is preparing his people for war. Our attitudes toward the devil should be, ENOUGH IS ENOUGH! It is time to get mad at the devil instead of each other. It is time for the Church to *WAKE UP!* For by doing nothing, we are losing the battle for our cities, our families, and our churches.

Know God, But Know The Devil, Too

I remember as a college football player in North Carolina, we practiced hours upon hours learning our opponent's plays and methods. We studied not just our own team's ways and strategies, *but also* the strength and weakness of each individual player of our opponent's team as well. We watched game films observing their every move. We set up plays on the practice field that resembled the plays of that upcoming opponent. We did all we could to know our opponent's every potential move and plan of action that could be used against us during game day. *Why?* Because our football team realized that if we studied our opponent's plays and the projected strategies they would use against us, *then we could form a "plan of action" to counter attack our opponent's actions, **thus winning the game!** Do you want to be a winner as a Christian?* It is time for us not to be deceived, we must know God, but we must also know our opponent as well — The Devil.

In the game of football, we had to know our own plays, but we had to know the plays of our opponent as well. In the same way, the Church must know God, but also know the strategies of the devil. Yes, it is important to know that God wants to heal you. Yes, it is important to know all the promises in the Word of God relating to prosperity, *BUT* it is just as important to know about your greatest opponent — the devil. Do you know the players on Satan's team? Have you seen the devil's "play book"? Do you know how Satan will attack you next? As leaders of God's people, *we need to know.*

Be thou diligent to know the *state of thy flocks*, and look well to thy herds.
Proverbs 27:23

I believe that David, even as a young shepherd boy, *was not deceived.* David knew the state of his flock. David knew how to protect his sheep from the bear and the lion. He knew how the bear and the lion "operated." I believe that David knew what rock the lion would "jump from" trying to kill his sheep. I believe David knew "in advance" which stone he would use in his sling to kill the bear if he attacked his flock. As church leaders, we must know how to protect our sheep. We cannot be deceived, we must not only know our God, but we must also know the "schemes" of the devil.

Satan Has An Army

For we wrestle not against flesh and blood, *but against principalities, against powers, against the rulers of the darkness of this world, against spiritual wickedness in high places.*
Ephesians 6:12

Satan has an army, but he is not God. We know that Satan is only a fallen angel. An angel is *not* omnipresent, "being everywhere at the same time." God is only omnipresent. So how does Satan "seem" to be everywhere at the same time. Satan has help. When Satan was kicked out of heaven, he took one-third of the angels with him (Revelation 12:9). He has an army with different rank and authority much like our military army in the United States.

In Satan's army there are privates, lieutenants, and captains, but they are under the authority of Satan. Unlike God's army, who operates in love, Satan's army operates in fear and hatred. God is a God who is our provider, but God is also our healer, advocate, and judge. There are many characteristics of God so, there are also many characteristics of Satan that we have to know and counteract. Remember, we stated earlier, it's not *if* Satan will attack you, but when and with what magnitude. We must be ready, but we must do more than just fight back. We must take the initiative and become offensive.

Satan Does Not Want To Be Exposed

Satan does not work by himself. He has a vast army. Satan and his army do not want to be found out. Satan does not want to be "exposed". Satan wants to lurk in the dark. As Christians, we are to "expose" the works of the devil and shed the light of the Gospel on them. It is our job to "expose" the works of the devil and then destroy them.

> **He that committeth sin is of the devil; for the devil sinneth from the beginning. For this *purpose the Son of God* was manifested, that he might *destroy the works of the devil.***
>
> **1 John 3:8**

Devils do not want you to know about them, or their ways. They do not want to be talked about. They do not want to be *identified*. And they surely do not want to be "bound" or "cast out."

6

Jesus, in His ministry, cast out demons. In fact, the majority of his ministry was in preaching (teaching), healing the sick (miracles), and casting out demons. Jesus was fully aware of Satan's kingdom.

And there was in their synagogue a man with an unclean spirit; and he cried out,

Saying, *Let us alone;* **what have we to do with thee, thou Jesus of Nazareth? art thou come to destroy us? I know thee who thou art, the Holy One of God.**

And *Jesus rebuked him,* **saying, Hold thy peace, and** *come out of him.*

And when the unclean spirit had torn him, and cried with a loud voice, he came out of him.

Mark 1:23-26

The demons in the man recognized Jesus and cried out, *"Let us alone."* The demons knew that Jesus could *expose them* and *cast them out from this man.* Once again, we are not here to glorify Satan, but we are here to *expose him* and to *destroy him,* making him ineffective in our lives. *Jesus came to destroy the works of the Devil.* You can have your nice little church services. You can sing nice little songs. You can save a few souls each year. *But* start "binding" spirits in the heavenlies and casting out devils, then all hell will break loose (Matthew 16:19). **You have now made the devil mad!** I want to be an earth shaker. I want to "walk" in Jesus' ministry. How about you?

The Promise of the Word is Not Automatic

In the introduction to this book, we discussed briefly that the concept of the promise in the Word is *not automatic.* The devil is a liar. He is a thief and robber. He did not obey God in heaven; why do you think he will voluntarily be obedient on earth? Satan has to be driven from your lives. Satan has to be forced out of your church. Satan has to be thrust out of your marriage and family. Trust me, he will not leave on his own. This is evident in the Body of Christ, as many are sick. The Word of God says that "by His stripes we are healed" (Isaiah 53:5), but why are so many of us sick and diseased? The promise is *not automatic*. We have to "demand" and "enforce" the rhema Word of God over our lives and families. Satan is an outlaw. We are God's sheriffs and we must enforce His law, the Word of God. One of the biggest deceptions by the devil is that bad things happen because God allows it. As a minister, people come up to me as I share the Gospel with them and they ask me, "If God is so loving why is there so much sickness and hatred here on earth?" I have heard this spoken so many times by non-Christians. I want to shake them and say "It is not God, but the devil." God's Word is true, but it is not "automatic" in our lives. God's laws "by faith" must be appropriated in our lives.

Do You Have Open Doors?

Many times as Christians, we open ourselves to Satan's attacks by the sin in our lives, or sin from past generations (sins of the father). If you have sinned or disobeyed, you must first renounce the sin and repent. But many times, Satan walks right into our lives and we say nothing. For example, if a man comes into my house and tries to harm my family and steal my possessions, I am not going to sit calmly by and let him do it. I am going to do whatever it takes to defend and protect my family. In the same way, the Church is being stolen from, raped spiritually, and looted, and as a Body, we are standing idly by, watching all this happen and doing nothing to defend ourselves, the Church. Jesus is coming again for a beautiful, pure and fully mature Church

(His Bride). He is not coming back for a spiritually impoverished Church, that has been robbed of *all* her Glory.

How is it that Satan is allowed to rob us? There are *three reasons*, (1) we are ignorant of the devil's devices, (2) we are apathetic, we just do not care (indifferent) or (3) we do not know how to fight back. I hope in this book you get *wise* to the devil, get off the bench, and become a soldier in God's army. You must enforce the promises of the Word in your life. You must take authority over the devil, put your spiritual foot down, and say, "you will not rob me anymore, Devil." God's promises are *not* automatic, you must enforce God's word or it will not get done. *It is that simple.* Sometimes we make things more difficult than they are. Once we know what to do, **JUST DO IT!** It is time for the Church of Jesus Christ to WAKE UP! It is time for the Church to not be *deceived* anymore.

He Could Not Be Stopped

Now when the *adversaries* of Judah and Benjamin heard that the children of the captivity builded the temple unto the LORD God of Israel;

Then they came to Zerubbabel, and to the chief of the fathers, and said unto them, Let us build with you: for we seek your God, as ye do; and we do sacrifice unto him since the days of Esarhaddon king of Assur, which brought us up hither.

But Zerubbabel, and Jeshua, and the rest of the chief of the fathers of Israel, said unto them, Ye have nothing to do with us to build an house unto our God; but we ourselves together will build unto the LORD God of Israel, as king Cyrus the king of Persia hath commanded us.

> Then the people of the land weakened the hands
> of the people of Judah, and troubled them in building,
>
> And hired counsellors against them, to *frustrate
> their purpose,* all the days of Cyrus king of Persia, even
> until the reign of Darius king of Persia (deceive them).
>
> And in the reign of Ahasuerus, in the beginning of
> his reign, wrote they unto him an accusation against
> the inhabitants of Judah and Jerusalem.
>
> Ezra 4:1-6

There are some interesting principals in this passage in Ezra. Here is a group of people who did not let the *weapon of deceit* slow them down. I am not advocating suspicion and distrust, but we have to be *spiritually minded.* As we seek to fill that spot on the church staff, we have to *discern* if that person sitting in front of us in an interview, has been sent from God or sent by the devil. As a minister, I have learned that people know how to say and act a certain way to sound religious. They can say the right words and act the right way, but their *heart is full of deceit.* Their motive is wrong. They have their own hidden agenda in mind and not the vision of the church or the "heart of God." I have learned the hard way. It is better to wait on the Lord to send the right man or woman, than hire the first person that claims to be qualified for the job.

As I was just beginning in ministry, I asked the Lord one simple prayer, "Lord if you have truly called me into ministry, then all I ask is that I will *never be deceived.* For if someone is telling me a half-truth, then through the gift of discernment, you would reveal the *truth* to me." God has been faithful over the years. For I learned that I cannot *discern* someone with my natural eyes, but I had to *discern* someone with my spiritual eyes.

Opposition Will Come

Now when the *adversaries* of Judah and Benjamin heard that the children of the captivity builded the temple unto the LORD God of Israel;

***Then they came to Zerubbabel,* and to the chief of the fathers, and said unto them, Let us build with you: for we seek your God, as ye do; and we do sacrifice unto him since the days of Esarhaddon king of Assur, which brought us up hither.**

Ezra 4:1,2

In this passage in the book of Ezra, it is interesting to note that the adversary *ONLY* attacked when Zerubbabel started building. In other words, if you are "playing church," you are not a threat to the enemy's kingdom, but once you decide to get serious with God, doing His will, not your own, then *watch out!*

When does Satan attack you with the *spirit of deceit*? ***When God's work begins!*** One young minister from North Carolina asked me if a "project" he was involved with was of God, or not? I quickly responded, "are you experiencing any opposition?" He said, "you would not believe how much opposition." I said, "you are in God's will." It is sad to see people stop a project of God when opposition arises. For they mistake opposition as a sign from God that "it is not God's will." But usually the opposite is true. The greater the work of the Lord, the greater the opposition. Sometimes God opens up doors, but sometimes God has called you to *"Kick the door open."*

An elderly woman came up to me and asked me why nothing bad ever happens in her life? I quickly came to the conclusion after asking her a few more questions she was doing nothing for God. Simply, she was not a threat to Satan's kingdom. In the *preparation period* of your ministry, God is *preparing* you for dealing with the opposition of the enemy. Since God knows the future, and what lies ahead for you, the "length of time" in the wilderness sometimes is determined by how you *defeat the enemy*. Before David went up against Goliath, he was successful *FIRST* against the bear and the lion. The Lord knows that your Goliath lies ahead of you. If you were successful in killing the bear and the lion, then God knows that you can also destroy your Goliath. Remember, the opposition came when the "building" began. Have you met your bear yet? Remember, the success you have with the "bear and lion" will determine your later success as you face your "Goliath."

Leaders — Watch Out!

Then they came to Zerubbabel, and to the chief of the fathers, and said unto them, Let us build with you: for we seek your God, as ye do; and we do sacrifice unto him since the days of Esarhaddon king of Assur, which brought us up hither.   Ezra 4:2

Who did the enemy approach *first*? Not only did the adversary attack when the "work began," but they attacked leadership. The attack came against the leader, Zerubbabel. Satan knows that the easiest way to take the greatest number of people away from a work of the Lord is by taking the leader out. Smite the shepherd, and the sheep will scatter. As leaders, we have to seek God for every person who is on our staff. We cannot take any position for granted. As leaders we have to place God's appointed people around us. But at the same time, we have to enlist "prayer teams" to hold us up before the Lord for Satan's desire is to attack the leader; thus, stopping the work of the ministry.

No Short Cuts

But Zerubbabel, and Jeshua, and the rest of the chief of the fathers of Israel, said unto them, Ye have nothing to do with us to build an house unto our God; but we *ourselves together* will build unto the LORD God of Israel, as king Cyrus the king of Persia hath commanded us.

Ezra 4:3

What did Zerubbabel and his elders do or *not do? They did not compromise.* Like a lot of churches, we accept anyone as members. That all sounds good and loving, but that is not what God said in his Word. It says that if a sinner with known sin will not repent, we should not even associate with him. That sounds so cruel. God is a God of love. God does love the sinner, *but hates the sin.* To get the job done we cannot compromise in any way.

I was at a revival in Texas and the audience consisted of about 100 people. The next day I read an article in the local paper about the meeting. It stated that the attendance was around 1000 people and 100 were saved. I was in the meeting and the attendance was not anything like that. When I asked the Evangelist why he had *exaggerated* the numbers to the press, he stated that by reporting large numbers, more people would come to the meeting and more people would get saved. The means does not justify the end. He was lying and *deceiving* the public. He was wrong and God would not honor the meeting. As leaders of God's people, we cannot be deceived by allowing the wrong people around us in our ministry and at the same time, we cannot compromise by conducting our ministries in an unethical way. We are many times tempted to take *short cuts* versus taking the longer road. A short cut is the path that gives the least resistance. As Christians, we have to constantly ask ourselves in all we do, *WHAT WOULD JESUS DO?* We cannot take *short cuts*, truly the ends do not justify the means.

But the *Gateway to Life is small,* and the road is narrow, and only a few ever find it.

Matthew 7:14 (TLB)

Many times the easiest way is not God's way. For example, God has spoken to you that you will be a pastor of a large church, but the road that leads there may be more difficult (different) than you think. You serve as an usher for two years and then later you can become a youth minister for another three years. You have had prophecy after prophecy during this time that you would have a large ministry and preach to thousands. Satan will whisper to you, "You do not need to serve under this pastor. Look at all his faults. You should start your own ministry *now.*" The *short cut* is very tempting. But if you take the short cut, you will produce an Ishmael ministry and not an Isaac. We have to wait on God and even though we do not understand or see the big picture, we have to trust God with our lives. What if Joseph took a short cut to gain power by submitting to the temptations of Potiphar's wife and sleeping with her? He was a 23 year old single man who still had the position of a Hebrew slave in Egypt. What an opportunity? But what did Joseph do? He refused the advances of Potiphar's wife (Genesis 39:8). What was his reward? He got thrown back into prison again. Even though Joseph did not know it at the time, he would later be used by God to save not just his own family during the famine, *but the entire Jewish nation.* His obedience and refusal to take the *short cut*, saved a nation.

Don't Be Deceived,
Have No Mercy on the Devil

And when the inhabitants of Gibeon *heard what Joshua had done unto Jericho* and to Ai,

They did work wilily, and went and made as if they had been ambassadors, and took old sacks upon their asses, and wine bottles, old, and rent, and bound up;

> And old shoes and clouted upon their feet, and old garments upon them; and all the bread of their provision was dry and mouldy.
>
> And they went to Joshua unto the camp at Gilgal, and said unto him, and to the men of Israel, *We have come from a far country: now therefore make ye a league with us.*
>
> **Joshua 9:3-6**

I do not want to pick on Joshua too much. He was a mighty man of God, but I wanted to show you an incident in his life when he did not seek God and thus, he was *deceived*. In the earlier part of this chapter, we looked at how Zerrubabel was successful in *discerning* that all the help that comes to us is *not necessarily* from God. However, Joshua, had some success as he entered into the promised land. The walls of Jericho have already fallen. After Achan's sin was discovered, Joshua was successful in destroying the city of Ai. One might say, "Joshua was on a roll, he had momentum on his side." Well, we all know that Satan does not come at you and say, "Hey, I am the devil and I have come to destroy you." The Devil is not that direct.

The Gibeon people were afraid of Joshua's success. They decided it was better to obtain peace (compromise) with them rather than fight. Even though the Gibeon people were not poor, they *tricked* Joshua by dressing in worn-out clothes and sandals. Joshua was looking at their physical appearance rather than seeking God to see their spiritual intent. Joshua looked (reasoned) with his natural eyes versus discerning the truth with his spiritual eyes. Joshua did not bother to seek God in regards to his decision (Joshua 9:14,15).

Why was it such a terrible thing to make peace with the Gibeon people? After all, doesn't God want us to live in peace with all men? But Joshua had a command

15

from God through his angel, "have no mercy on your enemy." When they defeated Jericho, everything was destroyed, men, women, young and old: oxen, sheep, donkeys — *everything*. This sounds so cruel today. In your Christian walk with the Lord, you must get this revelation. *God hates the devil.* Jesus' mission on earth was to destroy the works of the devil. We must realize today, that the war we are in is a *spiritual battle* not a physical one.

> *For we are not fighting against people made of flesh and blood,* but against persons without bodies — the evil rulers of the unseen world, those mighty satanic beings and great evil princes of darkness who rule this world; and against huge numbers of wicked spirits in the spirit world.
>
> **Ephesians 6:12 (TLB)**

When you read in the Old Testament of the Hittites, Amorites, Canaanites, Perizzites, Hivites, and Jebusites, these are symbolic of demonic forces. Joshua was ordered to have *no mercy* on the inhabitants of the land. God does not change. Just like the days of Joshua, we cannot have mercy on the devil either. We have to drive him out of our lives totally. We have to drive him out of our churches totally. We cannot make a peace treaty with him at all (Joshua 9:24). The devil does not play fair. His sole purpose is to destroy God's work and his people. He does not take any mercy on you. *You better not take any mercy on him. We cannot be deceived by making a peace treaty with the devil, for if you give him an inch, he will later take a mile.*

Delilah Deceives Samson

> And it came to pass, when she pressed him *daily with her words,* and urged him, so that his soul was vexed unto death;

That *he told her all his heart,* and said unto her, There hath not come a razor upon mine head; for I have been a Nazarite unto God from my mother's womb: if I be shaven, then my strength will go from me, and I shall become weak, and be like any other man.

And when Delilah saw that he had told her all his heart, she sent and called for the lords of the Philistines, saying, *Come up this once,* for he hath shewed me all his heart. Then the lords of the Philistines came up unto her, and brought money in their hand.

And she made him sleep upon her knees, and she called for a man, and she caused him to shave off the seven locks of his head; and she began to afflict him, and his strength went from him.

And she said, The Philistines be upon thee, Samson. And he awoke out of his sleep, and said, I will go out as at other times before, and shake *myself.* And he wist not that the LORD was departed from him.

But the Philistines took him, and *put out his eyes,* and brought him down to Gaza, and bound him with fetters of brass; and he did grind in the prison house.

Judges 16:16-21

First, how was Sampson deceived? Was this a one time encounter with Delilah? The word says that Delilah *"DAILY"* asked Sampson where his strength came from (verse 16). Sampson knew that Delilah was a prostitute. Sampson knew he should not be with her. *Over a period of time,* Delilah with her seducing and deceiving ways wore down Sampson. Many times the devil works this way. He will wear down your resistance, so eventually you stop praying. You stop going to church. You begin to isolate yourself, like a stray sheep, from the Body of Christ. And over a period of time your resistance to his attack is completely gone. You cannot "flirt" with sin...

for if you do, like Sampson, it can literally cost you your very life.

My wife and I had an opportunity to tour and minister in the Holy Lands. We traveled from the north as far as the Sea of Galilee and south to Jericho and the Dead Sea. In the southern region of Israel, is a famous battleground called Masada. During the Roman rule, all Jews were conquered except the Jews remaining in the fortress of Masada. If you have ever seen Masada, it is a large fortress on top of a mountain with tall walls. The Romans could not defeat the Jews with *conventional methods*. So they used a method called *"siege warfare."* What is *"siege warfare?"*

And I will camp against thee round about, and will *lay siege* against thee with a mount, and I will raise forts against thee.
Isaiah 29:3

Siege warfare is "the encirclement of a fortified place by an enemy with the intent of taking it" (Webster). In the war at Masada, the Romans formed circles around the Jews and over a period of time the food and water ran out. Eventually, a great ramp was made and the enemy came over the walls. The Jews were defeated and many people died.

In the same way, Satan will combat you with "siege warfare." In his *persistence*, he will try to gain control of your life, *by wearing you down*. By not tapping into God, your daily bread (word) and living water (prayer), you too will eventually die (spiritually) and be captured by the "deceiver." For instance, a Python snake surrounds its victims (siege) until the life is squeezed out of them. *Delilah nagged Sampson daily* (verse 16). She persistently, with her words, wore Samson down. *I said with her words.* Who said words cannot hurt you?

Death and life are in the power of the tongue: and they that love it shall eat the fruit thereof.

Proverbs 18:21

Delilah's consistency *with her words* eventually broke the man of God down. More than ever today, we must bring every "thought" captive to the obedience of God. We cannot "flirt" with sin, or Satan will say, "another one bites the dust."

And it came to pass, when she pressed him daily with her words, and urged him, so that his soul was vexed unto death;

That he told her all his heart, **and said unto her, There hath not come a razor upon mine head; for I have been a Nazarite unto God from my mother's womb: if I be shaven, then my strength will go from me, and I shall become weak, and be like any other man.**

Judges 16:16,17

Secondly, not only was Sampson deceived by the *"persistent words"* of Delilah, but Sampson was finally defeated by "totally" letting down all his resistance and gave up in his heart. What happens when you finally give in? What happens when all your resistance is gone? You are spiritually naked, you have taken off your "spiritual" armor.

Put on the whole armour of God, **that ye may be able to stand against the wiles of the devil.**

Ephesians 6:11

Be sober, be vigilant; because your adversary the devil, as a roaring lion, walketh about, seeking whom he may devour.

1 Peter 5:8

Samson had given up, or another way to put it, "he had given in to the devil." Sampson started spilling his guts. He shared all his heart with Delilah. This reminds me of people who drink alcohol. A perfectly reserved person at a social function can act like a total idiot with a few drinks in them. A person who cannot dance at all, dances up a storm when intoxicated. Similarly, sins that you have not acted on in a long time will resurface back up into your life.

> **And she made him *sleep* upon her knees; and she called for a man, and she caused him to shave off the seven locks of his head; and *she began to afflict him, and his strength went from him.***
>
> **Judges 16:19**

Have you become "spiritually asleep"? Are you "snoozing on the job" while the devil destroys your life? Samson went to sleep while the enemy was plotting to kill him (verse 19). When his life was getting ready to be destroyed, what did he do? *He went to sleep!* Likewise, Christians see their families being destroyed. We see our finances dwindling. We see our ministries being taken from us. What do we do? ***We go to sleep!*** Instead of "spiritually" sleeping, it is in these perilous times that we need to increase our prayer time, we need to meditate on the Word longer, we need to fast, we need to sit before Jesus' feet getting our marching orders from the King — King Jesus! *It is time for the church to wake up!* It is *not time* to sleep, *but fight!* We have to fight back and *"WAKE UP" TO THE SCHEMES OF THE DEVIL.*

> **But the Philistines took him, and *put out his eyes,* and brought him down to Gaza, and bound him with fetters of brass; and he did grind in the prison house.**
>
> **Judges 16:21**

Thirdly, what was the final blow? What did the Philistines do? They put out Samson's eyes. Why is this significant? If you cannot see (spiritually), you do not know where you are going. Saints, if you cannot see the attacks of the enemy, *you simply will lose*. If Satan can get you to be "blinded" to his devices and schemes, then you will not fight back. For example, instead of fighting the spirit of division that has been assigned against your marriage, you lash out at your wife. Instead of resisting the spirit of debt that has been assigned to destroy you financially, you stop tithing to make ends met. *IT IS TIME FOR THE CHURCH TO WAKE UP!* Let us quit fighting each other and God, and start *discerning* who the real enemy is, the Devil. Wake up Church! We cannot "flirt" with sin. We cannot "fall asleep" in the midst of the war. We cannot become "blinded" toward the schemes of the enemy. *It is time that the Church stops being deceived, and starts discerning the schemes of the enemy.*

The Deceitfulness of Sin

And the Lord said unto him, Now do ye Pharisees make clean the outside of the cup and the platter; but your *inward part* is full of ravening and wickedness.

Luke 11:39

Who me, deceived? You may say, "I have been a church member for years. My dad is even a pastor. I say and do all the right things." This is the attitude of many Christians. They are full of pride. They are sincere, but sincerely wrong. Many people who are born-again Christians are "blinded" to the ways of God and the will for their lives. We see the speck in our neighbor's eye, but cannot see the log in our own eye. This type of attitude is the manifestation of a religious spirit. This is one of the most evil, deceiving spirits. Jesus had to correct the Pharisees, "for their outward parts looked good, but their *inward parts (hearts)* were far from Him."

21

> *Having a form of godliness,* **but denying the power thereof: from such turn away.**
>
> **2 Timothy 3:5**

The spirit of religion has deceived many. This spirit looks like a Christian, says all the right words of a Christian, but simply, this "so called" Christian is not led by the Holy Spirit, but by their own carnal lust. Jesus was condemning the spirit of religion. The Pharisees were trying to obey the "law," but were far from God in their hearts, their *"inward parts."*

They knew the law, but not its "true meaning." *They were deceived.* When Jesus confronted them in regard to this, the spirit of religion then manifested. They wanted to kill Jesus. Jesus called them fools. He warned them, "Woe to you." He basically said, *"you have been deceived."* Sin can deceive our hearts. God wants to circumcise our heart and give us hearts after Him.

We have to be very careful that we are walking in the spirit of the law (Word) and not necessarily just by the letter of the law, for the letter kills and the spirit brings life. We have to be careful not to let the spirit of religion deceive us in thinking "we are God's gift to mankind" when we really are far from Him. Are you a modern day Pharisee? Are you deceived? *Let us all examine our hearts.*

Hardness of Heart

> **He hath blinded their eyes, and** *hardened their heart;* **that they should not see with their eyes, nor understand with their heart, and be converted, and I should heal them.**
>
> **John 12:40**

> **But exhort one another daily, while it is called To-day; lest any of you be** *hardened through the deceitfulness of sin.*
>
> **Hebrews 3:13**

What do I mean when I say "hard" hearts? We are not sensitive to our conscience anymore. We are not sensitive to the Holy Spirit. What used to bother us, does not bother us anymore. *We have become hardened to sin.* A good example, is the use of the illegal drug — cocaine. In the beginning, cocaine makes you feel good. But to make you feel the same way the next time, you need more. Your tolerance level increases in the amount of drug your body can handle. You eventually spend more and more money. It is one of the most addicting drugs there is. You are bound to it and you will do anything to maintain your habit. Sin deceives you in that once what you ruled, now rules you. You get hardened towards its effects and what once bothered you, now has no affect on you at all. *Your conscience is seared.* You have lost all sensitivity to the Holy Spirit.

Why is this *process* so deceiving? *It all happens so gradually.* In life, you have just veered off the road, next thing you know, you are in a ditch. You quit reading your Bible, next thing you know, you quit attending church. It is all a process. We have to be so careful that our hearts do not become hardened, but remain pliable to God.

The Pleasure of Sin

Why do most people hate Jesus and Christianity so much? Why did the religious leaders of Jesus' ministry hate Him so much? It is called confrontation! Jesus confronted the religious leaders of the sin in their hearts. He called them "Vipers and Fools." Hard words, yes, but Jesus told it like it was the hard truth. *Repent!* Why does the world hate the Christian, because the Christian way of life "convicts" the world of its sin.

Choosing rather to suffer affliction with the people of God, than to enjoy the *pleasures of sin for a season.*
Hebrews 11:25

23

I was sharing the Gospel with a young lady and she asked me, "Do you think there is life after death?" Part of my answer was this, "If I believe that this earth is all there is and there is not life after death and no Jesus, I sure would not be living a Holy life. I would be out having fun in the world and enjoying the *pleasure of sin*." But Praise God, there is life after death and I am going to be with Jesus in Heaven. How about you, are you going to spend the rest of your life pleasing Jesus or enjoying the temporal pleasures of sin? There is pleasure in sin, but it is only temporary leading to death and separation from God. One of the ways to help us maintain a Holy life that is pleasing to God, is to keep our minds focused on heaven rather than the temporary things of this world. We have to learn to hate sin, not people. We cannot focus on the temporary pleasure, but focus on the destruction and pain that sin causes. Lord help us hate what you hate and love what you love. Let us be spiritually minded, not carnally minded walking in the deceitfulness of sin (flesh). Lord, help us to not be deceived by the temporary pleasures of sin.

Your Greatest Weapon —
Gift of Discernment

One of the greatest weapons Satan uses today against the Church, is the spirit of *deceit*. Remember, we are not fighting against the person, but the spirit that is motivating the person (Ephesians 6). Our spiritual antennas should be up at all times. I did not say sometimes, but at **all times.** Even *one day* off (vacation from God) could be the fall of the ministry God has entrusted you to.

> **And it came to pass, after the year was expired, *at the time when kings go forth to battle*, that David sent Joab, and his servants with him, and all Israel; and**

they destroyed the children of Ammon, and besieged Rabbah. But David tarried still at Jerusalem.

And it came to pass in an eveningtide, that *David arose from off his bed,* and walked upon the roof of the king's house: and from the roof he saw a woman washing herself; and the woman was very beautiful to look upon.

2 Samuel 11:1,2

David should have been in battle, leading his men, but David decided to take a "day off." *It only took one day,* and David not only committed a sexual sin, but later committed murder as well.

Be sober, be vigilant; because your adversary the devil, as a roaring lion, walketh about, seeking whom he may devour.

1 Peter 5:8

We have to be on "call" 24 hours a day, 7 days a week. Satan does not take a day off — so you cannot either. We are walking in the end times, Satan realizes his time is short. We cannot pamper the flesh. He is waiting for you to take off your spiritual armor.

So, what is one of your greatest spiritual weapon that you can use to combat the schemes of the devil? It is utilizing your *gift of discernment.*

And he said, Take heed that ye be *not deceived:* for many shall come in my name, saying, I am Christ; and the time draweth near: go ye not therefore after them.

Luke 21:8

Remember, do not judge the authenticity of a Christian by the miracles, or signs and wonders they perform, but by the fruit of their life. Simply, you judge a ministry by a person's character, not the "so called" success of their ministry. As a pastor, I see so many young ministers so eager to walk into their ministries, but they do not want to *take the time* to let God develop their characters FIRST. *Do you want true success?* Well then, let God develop the *gift of discernment* in you. Take the time to let God develop true godly character in you. Learn the schemes of the devil, so you will not be *deceived* and stopped from fulfilling your destiny in life.

> For the time will come when they will not endure sound doctrine; but after their own lusts shall they heap to themselves teachers, having *itching ears.*
>
> 2 Timothy 4:3

> So God said to him, "since you have asked for this and not for long life or wealth for yourself, nor have I asked for the death of your enemies but for *discernment* in administering justice,
>
> I will do what you have asked. I will give you a wise and *discerning heart,* so that there will never have been anyone like you, nor will there ever be.
>
> Moreover, I will give you what you have not asked for — *both riches and honor* — so that in your lifetime you will have no equal among kings.
>
> And if you walk in my ways and obey my statutes and commands as David your father did, *I will give you a long life."*
>
> 1 Kings 3:11-14 (NIV)

We are in the last days. Jesus is coming back again soon. One of your biggest weapons against the *spirit of deceit* is the *spirit of discernment.* You must be tuned into God. You must be able to hear His voice. You must be able to tap into the spiritual world and see what God wants to reveal to you.

The world today is looking for anything that fits into their selfish agenda. They will be easily deceived and drawn away. In fact, even many of God's elect will be deceived. They will have itching ears. This is not a game. We must know the Word. We must know the signs of our times. We must have a *discerning spirit* and pray that the spirit of truth operates in our lives.

The man who *knows right from wrong and has good judgment and common sense* is happier than the man who is immensely rich! For such wisdom is far more valuable than precious jewels. Nothing else compares with it. Wisdom gives:

A long, good life, riches, honor, pleasure, peace.

***Wisdom is a tree of life* to those who eat her fruit; happy is the man who keeps on eating it.**

Proverbs 3:13-18 (TLB)

I like this translation of the Bible (The Living Bible) because it makes a clear statement. Happy is the man that finds discernment (knows right from wrong). He will have long life, riches, honor, godly pleasure and peace. And it goes on to say, "and he keeps on eating it." We have to keep after the things of God. And as the Word says, "to pursue peace, we also must pursue a *discerning spirit*. We will not know a man's ministry by his signs and wonders, but by the fruit of the spirit manifested in his life (Matthew 7:15-20). In the last days, we will have to discern a man's ministry by his character, not his signs and wonders.

As we *Cross the First Ten Yards* as we pursue our "calling" into our ministry, we must overcome the spirit of deceit. We must let God develop in each of us His discerning spirit. For as Adam and Eve were deceived at the "Tree of Life" destroying their future in the Garden of Eden, we must overcome this spirit of deceit right from the outset and pursue the *next ten yards towards our success — the spirit of doubt.*

Chapter 2
The Spirit of Doubt

Now the serpent was more subtle than any beast of the field which the LORD God had made. And he said unto the woman, *Yea, hath God said,* Ye shall not eat of every tree of the garden?

And the woman said unto the serpent, We may eat of the fruit of the trees of the garden:

But of the fruit of the tree which is in the midst of the garden God hath said, Ye shall not eat of it, neither shall ye touch it, lest ye die.

And the serpent said unto the woman, *Ye shall not surely die:*

For God doth know that in the day ye eat thereof, then your eyes shall be opened, and ye shall be as gods, knowing good and evil.

And when the woman saw that the tree was good for food, and that it was *pleasant to the eyes,* and a tree to be desired to make one wise, she took of the fruit thereof, and did eat, and gave also unto her husband with her; and he did eat.

Genesis 3:1-6

We saw in chapter one, how Satan deceived Eve. (Genesis 3:13). He deceived her and she ate of the tree of life that God told both Adam and Eve to not eat of. What was one of the ways that he tricked Eve? He made both Adam and Eve *doubt* the Word of God.

"Did God really say that?" (verse 1). The *spirit of doubt* is a powerful weapon used against the Body of Christ. If you do not gain victory over the *spirit of doubt* and "stand" on what you know from the rhema Word of God, you will never be used in a mighty way from God. Satan went on to say to Eve, "You shall not surely die." (verse 4). He basically was saying that God was a liar. You must not have heard it correctly. You cannot believe in the truth of the Bible. Remember, it was written by man, Satan was saying. According to Webster's dictionary, *doubt* is the *"wavering of opinion or belief"*. In other words, in your heart you are unsettled in regards to a matter. You are not grounded and your foundation is weak.

But when he asks, he must believe and *not doubt,* because he who *doubts* is like a wave of the sea, blown and tossed by the wind.

That man should not think he will receive anything from the Lord;

he is a double-minded man, unstable in all he does.

James 1:6-8 (NIV)

Let us look at how Satan uses the *spirit of doubt* against us and how we can fight back with the *spirit of faith.*

Warning Against *One Small* Word

And Jesus being full of the Holy Ghost returned from Jordan, and was led by the Spirit into the wilderness,

Being forty days tempted of the devil. And in those days he did eat nothing: and when they were ended, he afterward hungered.

And the devil said unto him, *If* thou be the Son of God, command this stone that it be made bread.

And Jesus answered him, saying, *It is written*, That man shall not live by bread alone, but by every word of God.

And the devil, taking him up into a high mountain, shewed unto him all the kingdoms of the world in a moment of time.

And the devil said unto him, All this power will I give thee, and the glory of them: for that is delivered unto me; and to whomsoever I will I give it.

If thou therefore wilt worship me, all shall be thine.

And Jesus answered and said unto him, get thee behind me, Satan: for *it is written*, Thou shalt worship the Lord thy God, and him only shalt thou serve.

And he brought him to Jerusalem, and set him on a pinnacle of the temple, and said unto him, *If* you be the Son of God, cast thyself down from hence:

For it is written, He shall give his angels charge over thee, to keep thee:

And in their hands they shall bear thee up, lest at any time thou dash thy foot against a stone.

And Jesus answering said unto him, It is said, Thou shalt not tempt the Lord thy God.

And when the devil had ended all the temptation, he departed from him for a *season*.

Luke 4:1-13

How does Satan breed "doubt and distrust" in the Body of Christ and in the Church? What did he do with Jesus as recorded in the book of Luke? He used *one small word*, "if." It is called **DOUBT**. "If" you are the son of God. "If" it is written. "If" it is true. Two of the ways that Satan tries to sow doubt is with the (1) infallibility of the Bible and with the (2) "calling" on a minister's life.

31

If Satan can get you to *doubt* that the Bible is *not* the infallible word of God, *you are walking on shaky ground.* I have heard ministers on Christian radio broadcasts try to promote their books and try to prove that a certain section of the Bible is not God. When man starts deciding in his own wisdom what is God and what is not, Christianity will fall. God's Word was written by man inspired by the Holy Spirit, not some of it, but *ALL.* You cannot pick and choose what you want to believe from God's Word. Satan will ask, "If the Bible is true, you cannot believe all of it, you are wiser than God. Remember, the Bible was written by man." Just like the scriptures above, Satan breeds *doubt by his words "if"* and he once again *misquotes* scriptures.

Secondly, Satan can try to get you to doubt your "calling." We all have a "calling" on our lives, whether in full time ministry or as a layman, we cannot let Satan get us to *doubt our "calling."* Have you ever heard of the "sent one" in the Bible? That is what I mean when I speak of someone who is "called" of God. You really have to *know* if you are "called" of God. *Why?* For when the "heat" is turned up in the frying pan, or the pressure of ministry is heavy, if you do not know *for sure* that you have been "called" to a task by God, *then you will fail.* Satan will hit you with his weapon of doubt, but if you *"know, that you know, that you know"* that you have been "called" of God, *YOU WILL HAVE VICTORY OVER THE SPIRIT OF DOUBT.*

As they ministered to the Lord, and fasted, the Holy Ghost said, *Separate me Barnabas and Saul for the work whereunto I have called them.*

And when they had fasted and prayed, and laid their hands on them, they *sent* them away.

Acts 13:2,3

Separate me Barnabas and Saul. Who separated them? It was not the men at the prayer meeting. It was the Holy Ghost. One of the best books I have read on the subject of God's will for your life, is Tim Storey's book, *A Good Idea or a God Idea?* The title of the book tells it all. Many of us are serving God in what we think God wants us to do. We are busy in our life doing the work of the ministry. But is it God's will for your life? Is it a good idea, or is it a God idea for your life? Are you achieving good things for God in your life or are you achieving God's *BEST* for your life?

I was reading my Bible during a lunch break in New Orleans, Louisiana; and little did I know, that my preparation period (wilderness) would last seven years before I started working in the ministry. The Lord sent me to serve under a minister in Fort Lauderdale, Florida. Then I moved to serve with a church in Asheville, North Carolina and then God *sent me* to serve with a mighty man of God in Chicago. What were my duties during those *seven years*? Well, I did not get to preach that much, but I was to *serve* the men of God who I was sent to. God was molding me and changing my *character*. It would not be the way that I would do it (my flesh was being crucified), but God had a plan for me. I could have started my evangelistic ministry that first year of my "calling." I could have started a church in New Orleans and help win more souls for the Lord. After all, we need more powerful churches in America. A good idea, but if I would have done either one of these "good ideas," *I would have been out of God's will.* I would have been operating in my own strength and not the "power and might" of the Lord.

"Then you will say, 'We ate and drank with you, and you taught in our streets.'

"But he will reply, *'I don't know you or where you come from.* Away from me, all you evildoers!'"

Luke 13:26,27 (NIV)

I cannot imagine doing any work (good idea) without God endorsing the work (God idea). Why is it important to know that you are "sent" by God? Why is it important that you know that you are *"called"* by God? Simply put, so you will endure. So you will "finish" the race God has put before you. *Remember, this book is to help prepare you for the race...so you will finish.* This book is to help you *Cross the Goal Line...Ten Yards at a Time.* Precept upon precept. Step by step. Inch by inch. Satan will attack your *"authority."* You must know your purpose. If God does not recognize you, Satan surely will not recognize you, when you try to attack him and his kingdom.

And the evil spirit answered and said, Jesus I know, and Paul I know; *but who are ye?*

And the man in whom the evil spirit was *leaped on them,* and overcame them, and prevailed against them, so that they fled out of that house naked and wounded.

Acts 19:15,16

The devil will leap on you and it will only be a matter of time before you will pack your bags and *run off like a dog with his tail between his legs.* We must know what *authority* we stand on. We must know that we are "called" and "sent" by God. As we know the Word in our heart, and we know God's will for our life, *we will not doubt.* We have to know who we are in Christ. We have to know our "identity" in Christ. We have to know our authority in Christ. We have to be *bold as a lion,* "walking by faith and not by sight." We must not be another victim to the "spirit of doubt", falling victim to one small word *"if"*.

The Double-Minded Man

If any of you lack wisdom, let him ask of God, that giveth to all men liberally, and upbraideth not; and it shall be given him.

But let him ask in faith, *nothing wavering*. For he that wavereth is like a wave of the sea driven with the wind and tossed.

For let not that man think that he shall receive any thing of the Lord.

A *double minded man* is unstable in all his ways.

James 1:5-8

It says that the Church is built on the *foundation of Jesus Christ*. The stone that the builders rejected became the cornerstone. The capstone of the Church. The key to the size of the building *depends on how strong the foundation is*.

For example, in Chicago, the tallest building is the Sears Tower. We all gaze upon the height of the building, *but what we do not see is how strong the foundation is, with cement poured several miles deep and wide*. The *spirit of doubt* tries to erode your foundation. The spirit tries to get you to question the basic foundation of the Gospel and what you believe. When one gets "saved", one of the first things we do for the new believer is take them through a "foundation class". It is so important that all Christians are grounded in the Word and really know what they believe. The Word says that you should always be ready to give an answer for what you believe. *We are to be prepared* (1 Peter 3:15). How can we be prepared if we do not know the Word. Our foundation must be firm.

A double minded man will receive nothing from God (verse 7). In other words, you cannot be unstable and expect anything from God. I heard a Christian counselor on the radio in Chicago say that, "About 90 percent of all Christians are confused. The reason is that we try to figure everything out." How true! What happened to *"trusting in the Lord, and lean not unto thy own understanding"* (Proverbs 3:5). What happened to walking by faith? What does it mean to be *double minded*? It means you are not sure of the situation. If someone asked you if the sky is blue, you would say "yes". The next day, another person asked you if the sky is red, you would say "yes". You are unsure, especially when you experience pressure coming to you from a particular situation. *It is like being a double-agent.* You work for the good guys and at the same time you work for the bad guys. You will not take a *"stand"* for anything. You are *tolerant* of everything, and can never establish any *"absolute truths"* in your life. God says, you will not get anything from Him. I don't blame Him. You cannot be trusted. We cry out to God to tell us the secrets of the universe and He cannot trust us with foundational issues yet. *We are unstable in all our ways.* Why does the devil have such great victory using the **spirit of doubt** against the leaders of God and His Saints? We do not know the "rhema" will for our lives.

You Must Make It Personal

How can we shoot at a target and strike it with accuracy, if we cannot see the target? How can we *cross the goal line,* if we do not know where the goal line is? My dad was a football player in high school. My dad is six foot four inches tall and weighs 250 pounds. He is a strong and large man. It still takes my two brothers and I to wrestle him to the floor. When I was a young boy, I remember him telling of a football player who recovered a fumble and ran all the way down the field for a touch down. What is so special about that story? We watch people run for touchdowns every weekend during the football season. This player recovered the fumble and scored a touchdown for the other team (safety). *He ran the wrong way.* He ran with all his might. He ran as fast as his legs would carry him, *but he ran the wrong way.* How many people strive at life and give it their all, just to find out at the end they were running the wrong way? Sincerity does not mean you are right. You can be sincerely moving in one direction, but sincerely running the wrong way. As Christians, Satan gets us to *doubt* God and his will for our lives, because we are not settled in our spirits about the matter. I am not saying settled in our minds, but our spirits.

What do you mean when you say to settle an issue in our spirits and not our minds? *Simply, you must make the issue personal...getting a "rhema" Word from God, not necessarily just knowing the "logos" Word.* What do I mean when I say "rhema"? What does "logos" mean? Rhema is a Greek word that means *"an utterance spoken specifically to an individual or collective group."* In other words, God specifically gives you or His church His will on a particular situation or matter. Logos is also a Greek word that means "something said." So, what is the difference? Very simply, "logos" is the written Word of God. It is "something said" by the Holy Spirit to the Body of Christ. The "logos" becomes "rhema" to you when the Holy Spirit "reveals" His will for you regarding a specific situation or decision, making His Word *"PERSONAL FOR YOU."* For example, God wants to relocate you and your family from Florida to Chicago. If you start searching the scriptures to find a verse that has the word Florida and Chicago in it, you will not find it.

Now what do you do? Many times, the Holy Spirit will lead you in the Word of God to scriptures that pertain to your move, which will be the *rhema* word of God for your personal situation.

I remember when I was in Asheville, North Carolina as a young minister and the Lord started dealing with me to move to Chicago. First of all, I was a southern boy and hated cold weather. Before I moved to North Carolina, I was living in Southern Florida. It was nice and warm (with no snow). I quoted the scripture, "delight thyself in the Lord and he will give you the desires of your heart." My heart's desire was to stay in the southern states. Well, God had other ideas.

For my thoughts are not your thoughts, neither are your ways my ways, saith the LORD.

For as the heavens are higher than the earth, so are my ways higher than your ways, and my thoughts than your thoughts.

Isaiah 55:8,9

In my prayer time each morning, the Holy Spirit started leading me to scriptures in the Bible that stated *"go north"*. I told the Lord, "that is probably not you." I told myself, "I probably am not hearing from God." Isn't it funny how you start *doubting* that you hear from God when your idea of how your life should go does not line up with God's way.

After several months, and seven scriptures telling me to *"go north,"* I finally got the word, the *rhema* on this move to Chicago. God later orchestrated some additional circumstances in my life and gave me a *peace in my heart* about the move. So, I moved to Chicago. By obeying the *"rhema"* Word, I married a beautiful woman of God from the Chicagoland area and now have two wonderful children. What if I did not obey the *rhema* Word of God?

I would have missed God's best for my life. It is so important that we know how to listen to God. It is so important that we not only know how to listen to God (rhema), but also act on what we know (obedience). It all takes faith. The *spirit of doubt* can really bring confusion about God, and what God has said, if you do not know how to receive the *"rhema"* Word of God. We might not understand how it is all going to work out, but when God says take a step on the water, by faith, we know it will either part for us to walk on dry land, or the water will hold us up so we won't sink. "For without faith, it is impossible to please God" (Hebrews 11:6). A double minded man is unstable in all his ways.

I asked myself, "should I move to Chicago or not? Should I take this new job or keep my present job? Should I start a new church in this part of town?" All good questions that have to be answered. God has the answers, but we have to know the *"rhema"* in regards to our *specific situation.* And if we do not, we will be wandering around aimlessly like a vagabond. We must overcome the *spirit of doubt* by knowing the *"rhema"* word for our specific situation, **God must make his will "personal" in your life.**

The Battle Ground is in the Mind

Wherefore gird up the loins of your mind, be sober, and hope to the end for the grace that is to be brought unto you at the revelation of Jesus Christ.

1 Peter 1:13

As we discuss the "double-minded" man, we have to look a little closer at where the battle lies. The Christian who *thinks* he is not in a battle is *deceived.* We are in a constant battle. Where is the battle ground for the individual Christian? *The battle ground is in the mind.* What does it mean to "gird up your mind"? When preparing to go into battle, the Roman soldier would pull up his pant-like garment and tuck it into his belt. He readied himself to do whatever it took to fight his opponent. His mind-set changed and his mind was now focused on *only one purpose*, to destroy his enemy. The Bible says that we are to be sober and alert. It did not say sometimes, but at *all times*. It is much like being on duty in the army, but with no R&R, rest and relaxation. We are never off duty. We even have to be careful what vacations we take as saints of God. One day away from God in your mind could be the end of the ministry that God has entrusted to you.

> **For to be carnally minded is death; but to be *spiritually minded is life and peace.***
> **Romans 8:6**

What does it mean to be spiritually minded? *We think like God.* How do you start thinking like God? You read and meditate on God's Word. You spend time with God and listen to what is on His heart. When you get saved, your spirit is renewed, but your *carnal mind has to be changed as well.* You cannot expect to hear from God watching soap operas everyday. You cannot expect to hear from God listening to secular music every day. We are in a constant battle over the desires of the flesh. We will reap what we sow. If we sow to the carnal mind, we will think like the world. If we sow to the things of God, we will start thinking like God. Our whole attitude will change. Faith will rise up in us. God's love and His fruit will start to be seen in our lives. *This change is not automatic.* We have to do something. We have a part to play.

> **And be not conformed to this world: but be ye**
> ***transformed by the renewing of your mind,* that ye may**

prove what is that good, and acceptable, and perfect,
will of God.

Romans 12:2

Let us win the battle over *doubt* by transforming our minds to the things of God. Let us start walking in God's blessing of "life and peace"and stop walking in doubt and insecurity.

Doubt Produces Fear

Wherefore I put thee in remembrance that thou *stir up* the gift of God, which is in thee by the putting on of my hands.

For God hath not given us the *spirit of fear;* but of power, and of love, and of a sound mind.

2 Timothy 1:6,7

We have seen where one word "IF" can cause you to stop in your tracks. We have seen where a DOUBLE-MINDED MAN will receive nothing from God. But there is a four letter word called "FEAR" that can paralyze the strongest of men. I once heard one preacher use an acrostic for F.E.A.R., *"Future Events Aren't Real."* How true! I mentioned that the battle ground is in the mind. When we are not sure of the "rhema" will of the Lord in a situation, or we are still waiting on God's intervention or direction concerning a matter, *fear can creep in.* Fear can cause you to turn back. Fear can cause you to *doubt the power* of God.

In the above reference scripture, Paul was encouraging young Timothy to "stir up" the gift in him. In other words, it was up to Timothy, *not God,* to keep marching forward. *Remember, the whole theme of this book, is not how you start the race, but how you finish the race.* Many men will start, but only a few will finish. Paul was saying to Timothy, "do not forget what is in you." The Holy Spirit lives within you. His power is

41

there. So "stir him up." Every time you try to go against the devil in the flesh, you will be defeated. But if you "stir yourself up", and say out loud, "greater is He (God) that is in me than he (devil) that is in the world," your spiritual chest will stick out. Boldness will rise up in you. And you will say to the devil, "make my day." We need to cop an attitude with the devil. We need to *stir up*" the gift within us.

What if we do not "stir up" God in us? Fear will rise up instead. God is looking for a yielded vessel through which His power can shine. He is looking for a man or woman who will not be stopped by the spirit of fear, doubting the power of God, the God of Abraham, Isaac, and Jacob. The God who created the earth and the God who is the King of Kings and Lord of Lords. I believe that God hates fear. I believe God is not pleased when his children doubt Him and draw back from the will of God in their life. Remember, without faith it is impossible to please God. Basically, God's hands are tied when we don't trust Him.

How is God going to put us in the game when we constantly live in fear and doubt? When Jesus was resurrected from the dead and approached Thomas, He showed Thomas His nail-scared hands to prove to him that it was truly He (Jesus) who came back to life.

Then Jesus told him, "You believe because you have seen me. *But blessed are those who haven't seen me and believe anyway."* **John 20:29 (TLB)**

We have to stand strong and keep our eyes on Jesus. We have to guard ourselves against the *spirit of doubt and fear*. It cannot rule in our lives.

Run For Your Life

There was a great prophet of God called Elijah. He was anointed and had performed mighty miracles of

God. Nothing could stop Elijah. He had just called fire down from heaven to kill 450 false prophets of Baal. But a few words from Jezebel caused this mighty man of God to flee into the wilderness with his tail between his legs. *The spirit of fear changed the whole disposition of the man.*

When Ahab told Queen Jezebel what Elijah had done, and that he had slaughtered the prophets of Baal,

she sent this message to Elijah: "You killed my prophets, and now I swear by the gods that I am going to kill you by this time tomorrow night."

So Elijah *fled for his life* [fear]; he went to Beer-sheba, a city of Judah, and left his servant there.

1 Kings 19:1-3 (TLB)

I always thought the timing of this event was amazing. Elijah had just experienced a great victory. The enemy was destroyed by God right before his eyes and before the dust settled, the words spoken by Jezebel caused him to flee. What happened to all of Elijah's faith? What happened to his confidence and his boldness? *The spirit of fear turned it all around.* We cannot under estimate the power of fear. If we mediate on the voice of Jezebel and not the word of God, we also will run. And God will say, what are you doing here in the back side of the desert? You should take on this woman just like you took on the 450 false prophets of Baal. There are two interesting principles here that need to be pointed out.

First, the spirit of fear attacks you hardest after your greatest victory. Satan attacks you when you are on top of the mountain, having just won a great spiritual victory. I remember, I had the opportunity to minister with a fellow minister in Kenya and Tanzania, East Africa. We had a tremendous meeting in both locations. God's power was evident as the Holy Spirit fell on the meetings. This was my first time in Africa. It was exciting, and was a life changing experience. I was home for only two days when I looked at my wife and said, "Sharon, I am so depressed. No one was saved today. No one was healed today. I am so unhappy." I caught myself and realized I was under attack. I could not live in the glory cloud all the time. I had to come down to the everyday life as well. It is fun to live and preach under the anointing of God, but what are you going to do when no one is watching you and your wife tells you to take out the trash and feed the kids on Monday morning? *It is called life.* You must be a real person. That is when the devil will whisper in your ear and say, "What's happened to all of your power now? God must not be with you anymore. The situation was a one time thing." The devil is a liar. He will speak *doubt and fear* into your life causing you to retreat like Elijah. The devil would love for you to forget past victories. He would love for you to forget how the Lord saved you and your entire family from disaster.

> So then *faith cometh by hearing,* and hearing by the word of God.
> **Romans 10:17**

What does the Word say, "Faith comes by hearing and hearing from the word of God." If we keep listening to the spirit of doubt, then like Elijah, we too, will be over-come by fear. Let us run the race for the long haul and not be side-tracked by the *spirit of fear.*

Second, the spirit of Jezebel must be "confronted" head on. If you do not confront this spirit, you will be defeated by fear and discouragement. I am talking especially to leaders who are called into the five fold ministry — *Apostles, Prophets, Pastors, Evangelists, and Teachers* (Ephesians 4). As spiritual leaders of God's Church...

sometimes we must use "tough love" dealing with this spirit of Jezebel. In seminary, I had a class on pastoral counseling called *nouthetic counseling*. Nouthetic counseling is a method of counseling that you confront the counselee head on in regards to the sin in their life as lead by the Holy Spirit. The one thing that I learned is that you have to be "direct and confront" the sin in people's lives. People, in general, do not like confrontation. We all want to be liked. We do not want to make people mad. We want to be tolerant of all things. We do not want to make waves. *But sometimes, we must deal with "sin" head on...telling the "truth in love." We cannot run from our problems, we have to stop and deal with them with the power of God.*

John the Baptist's main message was "repent." The religious leaders of the day hated John the Baptist and eventually cut off his head. John the Baptist was *confrontational*. He did not water down the message of the Gospel. He told it like it was. In the same way, the spirit of Jezebel has to be confronted and overcome. It will not go away. Many Christian leaders are avoiding the confrontation with the spirit of Jezebel. The Lord would say, "deal with the situation." Do not put it off any longer. Confront the problem head on, or *you too will flee for your life out of fear.* Stand up to that committee. Do not worry if the message you preach will cause your biggest financial supporter to leave the church. Do what God has put on your heart to do! *Just do it!* So be encouraged in the Lord. The sin of omission (doing nothing) can be a fatal mistake. If you know you should do something and then do not do it, that is sin. The world will not like you, but be confrontational. Are you a man pleaser, or a God pleaser? *Sometimes, the path to the **goal line** takes you straight through the mountain...not around it.*

I've Waited Long Enough

One of the most successful weapons Satan uses against the Church is the inability to *wait on the timing* of the Lord. When God is preparing to do something for us, it usually is not the way we thought it would come about, and definitely not the timing we would choose. The Lord says that a day to Him is like a thousand years, and a thousand years is but a day (2 Peter 3:8). As Christians, we seek God for His heart on a matter, but often we do not *wait for the timing* of God. Then we are disappointed when God does not come through in *our* timing. If we try to do it our way and not wait on God, then we end up with an Ishmael (good) instead of our Isaac (God's best). *The spirit of doubt will get the best of you, if you do not know how to wait on the timing of the Lord.* How do you wait on the Lord? What does God mean when He says to wait on the Lord? Why are we unsuccessful in waiting on the Lord? Let us answer these important questions.

(1) How Do You Wait On The Lord?

But those who wait on the LORD shall renew their strength; they shall mount up with wings like eagles, they shall run and not be weary, they shall walk and not faint.

Isaiah 40:31 (NKJV)

I see saints miss this very important principal so many times. Sometimes God just tells you to wait on Him and do nothing. I remember when God was teaching me how to receive from Him in the area of finances, the Lord told me *not* to take a job. That was hard for me, because I had always worked. I had to eat. In God's training techniques, *I had to learn that God was my source and not my job.* For a three month period, I did not work and God supernaturally supplied all my needs. This was a one-time experience in my life, and it was not the norm. Many times waiting on God is not sitting, but *actively pursuing* what you know is from God, and walking in that. In other words, keep doing what you are doing and what light God has shown you thus far regarding your situation. *Waiting is active, not passive.*

According to Webster's dictionary, wait means to *"be ready."* I like that definition. ***You are to be prepared.*** As a college football player, I wanted to be on the "first team" in my freshman year. But the coach said, "wait, your turn will come later." I could have just waited and sat on the bench. But during my waiting period, I got up early and worked out with weights. I ran extra laps to get in shape. I learned all the plays in the playbook. *I got prepared when no one was watching.* And when the coach said, "Hester, get in the game," I was ready. I seized the opportunity and became a starter. ***I paid the price when no one was looking or patting me on the back.***

In one of my counseling sessions with our church, a young Christian lady was so discouraged because God had not sent her mate yet. She seemed to be in distress. I learned that she had been serving God for years, but in her loneliness, she had *compromised* and was dating a young man who was not a Christian. She had fallen into sin. The Holy Spirit quickly prompted me to deal with her sexual sin and the *sin of doubting* God. She responded correctly to God, repented of seeking a man instead of God. Within a short period of time, God led her mate into her life. Our response to God can either shorten our waiting time, or increase it. *Your proper or improper response to God can either speed up your destiny or lengthen it.* Many times, God is just waiting for us to change. Remember, the Israelites journey was only 14 days, but it took 40 years to get to the promised land, and the parents still did not make it. They died in the wilderness.

(2) *Waiting is Active*

Waiting is active. Waiting on God is to keep doing what you know to do until you get another direction from the Lord. As the Lord says that He will direct our steps, I heard one preacher put it this way, "It is easier to lead someone when he is moving forward versus someone who is standing still."

My wife and I were looking for a new place to live. God had shown us it was time to move into a larger house. Every weekend my wife and I looked at homes. The place we were living in was already sold, and we had only a few weeks to find a new place to live. We had been looking for months, but had been unsuccessful in finding a place. *We were actively "waiting" on God.* We were doing what we knew to do. Two weeks before we had to move, a business associate told me that he had bought a new home and asked me if we wanted his house. It was perfect. It was larger, in a good location, and the price was right. As we were waiting on God, actively looking for homes, God led us to the perfect house. We were not just in our prayer closets asking God for a home. Sometimes God says to do that, but usually God says to *"actively"* wait on Him.

(3) *Why Do We Fail On Waiting For God?*

Why are so many of us unsuccessful in waiting on the Lord? How does the *spirit of doubt and unbelief* work against us when we are waiting on the Lord? We have already mentioned that you have to know the heart of God on your situation first, *"RHEMA"*. But once He gives you his will regarding a matter, what next? We usually try in our reasoning to figure out how God will come through. When you read the Bible and look at your own life, His timing and His way are usually different from yours.

> *For my thoughts are not your thoughts,* neither are your ways my ways, saith the LORD.
>
> *For as the heavens are higher than the earth, so are my ways higher than your ways, and my thoughts than your thoughts.*
>
> **Isaiah 55:8,9**

We think that we know God's purpose in all of the areas of our lives, but we only know one piece of the puzzle. He made the puzzle. He knows the beginning from the end. He is the Alpha and the Omega. *HE'S GOD AND YOU'RE NOT!*

I was in a Christian Conference held by Dr. Bill Hamon in Destin, Florida, and I heard Dr. Hamon put it like this: "When you are seeking God's will on a matter, a good way to remember it by is the three W's method." Simply, God's will can be judged in three areas. *First*, does it line up with the Word of God? (**Word**). *Secondly*, is it God's will — His *rhema* regarding you individually? (**Will**). *Thirdly*, is it God's way, His timing? (**Way**). For example, it is much like coming to a traffic light. You are stopped at the intersection waiting for the light to turn green (Word), but this time before the green light, the light turns yellow — the caution light (Will). This light tells you to get ready to go. The final light this time is green which means to go (Way). You push the gas and you move out. It's much the same way, when you are seeking God. In the Word, God gives you a "rhema" regarding His will on the matter (Word and Will), but this doesn't mean God has said to go yet. *He is telling you to get ready to move in His timing*. Finally, God says, "*Go*". Only then do we go. Waiting on God is not easy.

It takes real discipline with the help of the Holy Spirit. As a minister, I see so many saints of God miss it in this crucial stage — **WAITING ON GOD**. The *spirit of doubt* can cause you to miss God's best for you and your ministry. Let us look at a few situations in the Word to find out why people fail to wait on the Lord.

(4) Saul Could Not Wait

King Saul was a mighty man of God. He was anointed and appointed by God. But King Saul lost his throne. *Why*? He disobeyed God. What would cause a man to lose his position as king? *He did not wait on God.*

> And Samuel said, What hast thou done? And Saul said, Because I saw that the people were scattered from me, and that thou camest not within the *days appointed*, and that the Philistines gathered themselves together at Michmash;
>
> Therefore said I, The Philistines will come down now upon me to Gilgal, and I have not made supplication unto the LORD: *I forced myself therefore, and offered a burnt offering* [could not wait].
>
> And Samuel said to Saul, *Thou hast done foolishly:* thou hast not kept the commandment of the LORD thy God, which he commanded thee: for now would the LORD have established thy kingdom upon Israel for ever.
>
> **1 Samuel 13:11-13**

Samuel had commanded Saul to *wait* seven days for him to arrive. Saul was not to go out to battle until Samuel arrived. In Saul's disobedience, he not only did not wait on the Lord, but he committed a second sin by offering the sacrifice to the Lord which was only reserved for Samuel.

Why did Saul disobey God by not waiting? In verse 11, why did Saul say, "You did not come in the appointed time?" In fact, Samuel did come on time, but it was at the very end of the time period he had commanded Saul to wait. *I found it true in my life that God usually waits until the last moment.* He wants to stretch our faith, and in this I believe God also gets the most Glory. I will even go on to say, *"the more mature you are in the Lord, the longer many times you have to wait for His perfect will."* For instance, suppose God has told the leaders at your church that the new church building will come to pass this year. We do not see anything happening in the natural (after about 11 months). So, we go out in our own reasoning and obtain a mortgage to build (not waiting on God's way, or timing). God had a different plan. God wanted to give us a building with no strings attached. But because we missed God's *way, timing, and heart* (by not waiting), we purchased a church building, *we would have received the good of God and not the BEST.* For if we had waited, God had a man prepared to give us the whole amount without taking out a loan. God had a plan to give us a new building — *FREE.* Can you see how we miss God so much in the big and small things of life? Let us choose to wait on God...for it is true in saying, *"IT IS ALWAYS BEST TO WAIT ON THE ALMIGHTY, FOR HE ALWAYS HAS THE BEST FOR YOU, IF YOU ONLY WAIT."*

We so many times try to figure out the answer. We try to figure out the way God is going to come through, and when it seems that God is not coming through, well around the corner walks Samuel and says, "What have you done?"

Saul not only tried to figure God out (Proverbs 3:5), *but he let peer pressure get the best of him.* He took his eyes off God and started listening to deacons: "We really need a new place, pastor." "What are we going to do?" "I need an answer now." "Aren't you going to do something?" As a minister, you really only have one person to answer to, *that is God*. Whom are you trying to please, man or God? I have seen so many strong men of God miss it in this area. We start focusing on the need rather than the God who has the answer to the need, in his timing.

> **For the revelation awaits an appointed time; it speaks of the end and will not prove false. Though it linger, *wait for it; it will certainly come and will not delay*.**
>
> **Habakkuk 2:3 (NIV)**

It is easy to be strong and courageous when all is going well, but you will find out how strong you are in the Lord when *"all hell breaks loose."* In marriage counseling, one lady came up to me and said, "he was not like that before we got married." Marriage has a way of putting *pressure* on you, thus revealing the true you. Marriage is one of God's refining processes. When the junk (un-godliness) in your life is revealed, it is God's way of telling you that you need God to clean up that area of your life. Waiting on God? *It is not as easy as you think, but it is a vital test that you must pass before you can walk into the ministry that God has for you.*

Saul did not pass the test, but we can learn from his mistakes, and walk in victory — AS WE WAIT (NOT DOUBTING) FOR THE LORD!

(5) Sarai Could Not Wait

The wife, of father Abraham, was a woman of God. She was honored by God and her husband. She was the mother of the nation of Israel, *but Sarai missed it with God.* What did Sarai do to hurt God? *She did not wait on the Lord*. She *doubted* that God could perform what He had promised. So she thought, *that God needed help!* That is the problem with many of us today, *we thought*.

> **Now Sarai Abram's wife bare him no children: and she had an handmaid, an Egyptian, whose name was Hagar.**
>
> **And Sarai said unto Abram, Behold now, the LORD hath restrained me from bearing:** *I pray thee, go in unto my maid; it may be that I may obtain children by her* [her idea not God's idea]. **And Abram hearkened to the voice of Sarai.**
>
> **Genesis 16:1,2**

Now Sarai (later Sarah) in her thinking *reasoned*, since she was sterile and could not have a baby, that *God needed help*. She was past her years to have children. Could God really come through? God had already promised her and her husband Abraham that he would be the "father of many nations." He told Sarai that she was going to have a child, well, she "laughed" at God. She was basically saying to God, "No Way!" Because Sarai did *not wait* on God, Hagar did have Ishmael when God wanted an Isaac (good idea, but not a God idea). God did visit Abraham. Thirteen years after Ishmael was born, God visited Abraham and said, "*It will come to pass (my way)."*

I was attending a conference in Chicago and watched as Dr. Tim Bagwell gave the "Word of the Lord" to people within the meeting. I witnessed the "joy" that the people received as the Word of the Lord was spoken over their lives. New strength and courage were received to keep up the good fight of faith. New vitality and hope were received to keep the eyes of God's people on Him and not their circumstances. Does not the Word of God say in regards to prophesy, "that it is for edification, exhortation, and comfort?" (1 Corinthians 14:3). As Sarai could not believe God to do what He had promised and wait on Him to perform it, *sometimes just a simple "comforting" Word from God can make the difference from either an Ishmael or Isaac for your life.* We all need encourage-ment. And many times, God uses us to spiritually put our arms around someone and say, "It will surely come to pass."

The *spirit of doubt* can literally destroy you if you do not overcome it. Adam and Eve were kicked out of the Garden of Eden for one small word called *"if"*. A great man of God (Elijah) ran for his life from *words of fear* from Jezebel. Saul *doubted* God by *not waiting* on Samuel losing his throne. *How about you...have you overcome the spirit of doubt...as we get "TEN YARDS" closer to our GOAL LINE?* One of your key spiritual weapons in overcoming the spirit of doubt is *FAITH*. As we close this chapter on the "Spirit of Doubt"...*let us put on the mantle of "faith" as we discard the garment of "doubt."*

The Spirit of Faith

But *without faith* it is impossible to please him: for he that cometh to God must believe that he is, and that he is a rewarder of them that diligently seek him.

Hebrews 11:6

The spirit of doubt is a powerful weapon used by Satan if you allow him to use it against you. Many great men and women of God have gotten side-tracked or stopped by this spirit. As children of the King, we do have a weapon that is mighty. It is called the *"spirit of faith."* In my counseling sessions, one of the hardest answers to give someone is, "I do not know (God has not revealed it yet) and you are just going to have to wait on God."

So then faith cometh by hearing, and hearing by the word of God.

Romans 10:17

God knows that we all need encouragement at times. That is why He told us to read the Word. Not one time. *But over and over again.* We must hide it in our hearts. *Why?* So we will not forget it when we need it — when Satan attacks us with the spirit of doubt. God wants us to get His Word from our heads (minds) down into our spirits. The *spirit of faith* is a strong counter weapon to use against the spirit of doubt, but we must exercise our weapon and be ready to use it when we need it. The time to stand to exercise your faith is not when tragedy strikes, *but before it strikes...NOW!* You should already have the Word of God in your spirit now. The time to exercise your faith when financial tragedy comes is now, not later when you are already in the "pits of debt." Like a substitute player waiting to get in the game, so we must be ready at all times to exercise our faith. Delays will come. Adversity will come.

> *Many are the afflictions of the righteous:* but the LORD delivereth him out of them all.
>
> Psalm 34:19

It is not if adversity comes, but when. Is your faith muscle strong? Are you ready to overcome the spirit of doubt with your weapon of faith? The time is now, not later...to build your faith muscle to have victory in your life, as you *Cross the Goal Line...Ten Yards at a Time.*

> Cast not away therefore your confidence, which hath great recompense of *reward.*
>
> For ye have *need of patience,* that, after ye have done the will of God, ye might receive the promise.
>
> For yet a little while, and he that shall come will come, and *will not tarry.*
>
> *Now the just shall live by faith:* but if any man draw back, my soul shall have no pleasure in him.
>
> Hebrews 10:35-38

I don't know about you, but I am going to sacrifice and pay the price of obedience to God; I want to get the praise of God. I want my reward. I will finish the goal line and receive my incorruptible crown. *Praise the Lord!* I want all that God has for me. I do not want to lose one reward reserved for me in heaven. That should be your desire too, if you play, let us play to win.

I hear saints tell me, *"it is so hard to wait."* I say, *"God's best is worth waiting for."* During the waiting time, we are getting equipped. We are getting prepared for ministry. We are building our foundations strong and deep. We are building the character of Jesus in our lives. Are you being overcome by the spirit of doubt, or are you building your faith muscle to withstand the test of time? Obtain victory as you finish the job for the Lord.

> **He is like a man which built an house, and digged deep, and** *laid the foundation on a rock:* **and when the** *flood arose,* **the stream beat vehemently upon that house, and** *could not shake it: for it was founded upon a rock.*
> **Luke 6:48**

Not only do you have to jump the hurdles of deceit and doubt, but you must have victory in the area of *discouragement* as well, to obtain the "high call" of your life.

Let us now explore in the next chapter, the *"Spirit of Discouragement"*.

Chapter 3
The Spirit of Discouragement

And they heard the voice of the LORD God walking in the garden in the cool of the day: and Adam and his wife *hid themselves* from the presence of the LORD God amongst the trees of the garden.

And the LORD God called unto Adam, and said unto him, Where art thou?

And he said, I heard thy voice in the garden, and *I was afraid,* because I was naked; and I hid myself.

And he said, *Who told thee that thou wast naked?* Hast thou eaten of the tree, whereof I commanded thee that thou shouldest not eat?

Genesis 3:8-11

As we continue to look at Satan's "Top Ten Hit List" of weapons to stop, divert, or slow you down in God's plan for your life, the *"spirit of discouragement"* is once again a powerful weapon used by Satan's team to hurt the Body of Christ. When you get discouraged, you have a tendency to get your "focus" off of Jesus and onto situations, or problems of life. As I was starting to write this chapter, the word EXPECTATION came to mind. *When you expect something to happen a certain way, in a certain time frame and it does not happen, you can become discouraged.* Satan loves to discourage God's people. He whispers in their ears "God did not really mean that." He says, "It might work for somebody else, but it will not work for you." You might be thinking, Pastor, you do not understand my situation, God cannot help me. Satan is a liar. When Adam had eaten the fruit from the tree of life he knew he had done wrong and he was afraid. Both Adam and Eve tried to hide from God. When we do wrong, even when we know what is right, we can get discouraged. Satan bombards our minds with feelings of guilt and shame. We reason in our mind, "there is no help for me now, I really did all those wrong things." God loved us so much even while we were yet sinners. Jesus still loves us. There is not one thing we can do that will separate us from the love of God.

> *Who is he that condemneth?* **It is Christ that died, yea rather, that is risen again, who is even at the right hand of God, who also maketh intercession for us.**
>
> *Who shall separate us from the love of Christ?* **shall tribulation, or distress, or persecution, or famine, or nakedness, or peril, or sword?**
>
> **Romans 8:34,35**

Let us look at ways that the *spirit of discouragement* has affected many men of God in the Bible. What are some of the reasons we get discouraged? How can we prevent this spirit from hurting us or our fellow believers?

Keep Your Eyes On Jesus

We all know the story of Jesus' disciple, Peter. I call him bold Peter. Right or wrong, he was always the first one to speak out and say, "nothing can stop me from following you, Jesus." Remember, he was the first to walk on water and he was the first to defend Jesus in the garden by cutting off the ear of the Roman soldier as they were going to take Jesus to be crucified. Also, Peter was the one who boldly proclaimed that he would never deny Jesus. After the Roman soldiers took Jesus, Peter denied Jesus not once, but *three times. You talk about one discouraged man! In fact, he wanted to kill himself.*

And he said, *Come.* And when Peter was come down out of the ship, he walked on the water, to go to Jesus.

But *when he saw* the wind boisterous, he was afraid; and beginning to sink, he cried, saying, Lord, save me.

***And immediately Jesus* stretched forth his hand, and caught him, and said unto him, O thou of little faith, wherefore didst thou doubt?**

Matthew 14:29-31

When Peter obeyed Jesus and stepped out of the boat, it took some real faith. I remember when my wife and I were in Israel, we had the pleasure of taking a boat similar to the one Jesus and Peter took many years ago. The unique aspect about the sea of Galilee is that it can be completely calm and within a few minutes, a terrible storm can emerge. It reminds me of when I lived in South Florida. People would say, "if you do not like the weather just wait a few hours." When Peter walked on water, the water was not calm, because of a terrific storm. The waves were high and the wind was howling. Many things were fighting for his attention. The circumstances looked pretty bad. But what did Peter do? Jesus did not have to coach him or give him three reasons why he should step out of the boat. Jesus simply said, "Come!" Peter instantly stepped out on the water. Amazingly, he did not sink. In fact, Peter was walking on water. But what happened? Peter started looking around him. He started focusing on the waves and the strong winds. *His eyes got off of Jesus and onto his surroundings.* Peter became afraid. Faith was dispelled and fear arose. Peter began to sink.

What do I mean when I say, "keep your eyes on Jesus"? Jesus was resurrected on the third day. Jesus is in heaven now. How do we keep our focus on him? I heard one of my favorite evangelists, Tim Storey, put it this way: "God is the potter and we are the clay." Each one of us is uniquely formed and made by God. God has a special plan for our lives. As special as Tim Storey is, I cannot be Tim Storey. I am Marcus Hester. You are who you are. God does not make mistakes, you are wonderfully made, you have been made by God. God wants me to be all Marcus Hester can be in what He has called me to do. Yes, I can learn from others, but I am to be me. I must be focused on what God has called me to do in my stage of my life. Are you in God's will? Are you allowing God to work through the uniqueness of who you are in Christ? Or are you trying to walk in the "calling" of someone else?

As we get focused on something other than what God wants for us, we allow the *spirit of discouragement* to gain a stronghold in our lives. We become critical and resentful of others. The spirit of jealousy works along with this spirit. We see others promoted before us. We see others getting what we are praying for. If we are not careful, bitterness and resentment can creep into our hearts. Remember, man looks on the outward appearance, but God looks upon the heart of the man. We have to guard our hearts lest Satan gains a foothold in our lives. We must keep focused. We must keep our eyes on Jesus, *on the "calling" for our lives, not someone else's.*

As God was molding Peter, God loved the boldness of Peter. I believe the Spirit of God has a hard time working through fearful people. God is looking for men and women of faith. It is impossible to please God without faith. Peter had faith and boldness, but God had to show Peter how to walk in the Spirit, and not in the flesh. When Peter started sinking, what happened? *IMMEDIATELY*, Jesus stretched out his hand to save Peter. Let us keep focused. Keep on keeping on! Do what God told you to do and not what he told someone else to do. In Tim Storey's book, *A Good Idea or God Idea*? It is a good idea to start a church, but is it God's idea for you. We really have to learn how to wait on the Lord and do his will. Keep focused and having done all, stand.

One lady came up to me and said, "What should I do?" I said, "keep doing exactly what God has shown you to do until he gives you further direction." Walk in the light and keep doing what you know to do. That is waiting on the Lord. We must keep focused and not let the *spirit of discouragement* side track us in our walk with God.

Shattered Dreams

And it came to pass after these things, that his master's wife cast her eyes upon Joseph; and she said, Lie with me.

But he refused, and said unto his master's wife, Behold, my master wotteth not what is with me in the house, and he hath committed all that he hath to my hand;

There is none greater in this house than I; neither hath he kept back any thing from me but thee, because thou art his wife: how then can I do this great wickedness, and sin against God?

And it came to pass, as she spake to Joseph day by day, that he hearkened not unto her, to lie by her, or to be with her.

And it came to pass about this time, that Joseph went into the house to do his business; and there was none of the men of the house there within.

And she caught him by his garment, saying, Lie with me: and he left his garment in her hand, and fled, and got him out.

And it came to pass, *when she saw that he had left his garment in her hand,* and was fled forth,

That she called unto the men of her house, and spake unto them, saying, See, he hath brought in an Hebrew unto us to mock us; he came in unto me to lie with me, and I cried with a loud voice:

And it came to pass, when he heard that I lifted up my voice and cried, that he left his garment with me, and fled, and got him out.

And she laid up his garment by her, until his lord came home.

And she spake unto him according to these words, saying, The Hebrew servant, which thou hast brought unto us, came in unto me to mock me:

And it came to pass, as I lifted up my voice and cried, that he left his garment with me, and fled out.

And it came to pass, when his master heard the words of his wife, which she spake unto him, saying, After this manner did thy servant to me; that his wrath was kindled.

And Joseph's master took him, and put him into the prison, a place where the king's prisoners were bound: and he was there in the prison.

But the LORD was with Joseph, and shewed him mercy, and gave him favour in the sight of the keeper of the prison.

Genesis 39:7-21

We all know the story of young Joseph and his betrayal by his brothers as he was sold into slavery in Egypt. Even though Joseph was in a foreign land and far away from his family, he was trying to make the most of a bad situation. In fact, he was doing pretty well. Joseph's master was well pleased with him and made him overseer of his house. What an honor for a Hebrew slave. It seemed like things were getting better. His brothers in their jealous hatred, sold their youngest brother into slavery, but Joseph was going to make the best of a raw deal. So what happened? Satan started using Potiphar's wife to try to seduce Joseph. Joseph, in his love for God and his master, would not have anything to do with her. *Joseph was falsely accused* and thrown back into prison. That does not seem fair to me. I can hear Joseph now: "God, I am serving you and doing the things you wanted me to do and you pay me back like this?" "What is up, God?" Joseph did not know that years later he would be used by God to save the whole nation of Israel from famine. Joseph only knew one thing, He was serving God and now He was back in prison, falsely accused.

I would say Joseph's dreams now were *finally shattered*. Instead of going forward and being restored by God, it seemed that things were going backwards. I do not know why God only shows us parts of the puzzle of our lives at times, but He does. It says even as we prophesy, that we only prophesy in part. We only see part of the overall picture of our lives. Why does God do this?

One reason, God wants to know if we really trust Him as our Lord. Do we really trust Him with our lives? I believe if God showed us too much at a time, we would not be able to handle what He is doing in our lives. We probably would miss our destiny. It is as simple as that. *Why do we get discouraged?* Why do we move along with the things of God and all of a sudden we let the *spirit of discouragement* get a hold of us? We allow the *spirit of discouragement* to take hold when we **EXPECT** something to happen in our time frame and it does not happen. Your *expectations* do not come to pass. I see this so many times as a minister. For example, one expects a certain behavior from his pastor, but his pastor disappoints him.

One lesson I learned early on in ministry is people will let you down, but God never will. That does not mean we can never trust one another, but what I am saying is, we must keep our focus on Jesus and not the person.

I remember as a small boy, when my dad said that he was going to take me to Disney World the following Saturday, I did not doubt him; I did not worry about it. My dad would come through. In today's society of the absent father in the home, our children have been so disappointed by people that say they love them. They learn not to expect anything from anyone, much less God. *Much like Joseph, our dreams have been shattered.* Our expectations have not come to pass. **We have been disappointed.** We have been hurt by people. We have been offended. Life has not gone the way we thought it would go. People have let us down. It seems like God has let us down. The *spirit of discouragement* can really take hold when we try to figure out God with our own reasoning.

> **Trust in the LORD with all thine heart; and *lean not unto thine own understanding.***
>
> **In all thy ways acknowledge him, and he shall direct thy paths.**
>
> **Proverbs 3:5,6**

God does have a plan for our lives, but God will *reveal* the will for our lives in His timing. If we do not trust God (trying to figure it out in our own reasoning), we then open ourselves up to being prey for the root of discouragement to get a foothold in our lives

It looked like Joseph's life was over. As we know, at the end of the story, Joseph saved his whole family. Satan thought that he really had destroyed Joseph, especially when he was falsely accused by Potiphar's wife. *Joseph could have gotten really discouraged. But what did Joseph do?*

> **But the LORD was with Joseph, and shewed him mercy, and gave him favour in the sight of the keeper of the prison.**
>
> **And the keeper of the prison committed to Joseph's hand all the prisoners that were in the prison; and whatsoever they did there, he was the doer of it.**
>
> **The keeper of the prison looked not to any thing that was under his hand; because the LORD was with him, and *that which he did, the LORD made it to prosper.***
>
> **Genesis 39:21-23**

Even in prison, God was with Joseph. In other words, whatever Joseph put his hands to, he would always rise to the top. He could not be held down. In prison, Joseph still prospered. What an anointing on Joseph's life! Joseph did not let the *spirit of discouragement* keep him down. He might not have understood everything God was doing, but he made the best of every situation whether good or what SEEMED like bad. Finally, Joseph saw his youngest brother, Benjamin, and his aged father, Jacob. Satan meant it for evil, but God meant it for good, to save the whole nation of Israel from famine.

> **But Joseph said to them, "Don't be afraid. Am I in the place of God?**
>
> **You intended to harm me, but God intended it for good to accomplish what is now being done, the saving of many lives."**
>
> **Genesis 50:19,20 (NIV)**

Joseph trusted God even when it looked like his whole life was one big *SHATTERED DREAM*. How about you? Are you trusting God even when your natural circumstances don't seem to line-up with your dreams? Are you overcoming the *spirit of discouragement* in your life? Are you allowing God to turn your situation around, turning the bad into good? God is faithful. As we mature in the Lord, we cannot let the *spirit of discouragement* slow us down in the things of God.

Why Does Satan Fight A Word of Prophecy?

The Lord led me to a mighty man of God, Dr. Bill Hamond. Bill had started a ministry called, *Christian International* in Santa Beach, Florida. He had a vision of a large training center even though there was nothing around him in the way of people, or buildings. Today, the vision has come to pass and Dr. Hamond is training and equipping many in the flow of the prophetic. Praise God! He did not let anyone stop him from fulfilling the dream that God had given him. But why would Satan fight this movement so hard? How does the *spirit of discouragement* relate to the prophetic word from God?

Many in the Body of Christ believe that prophecy was abolished with the life of Paul, but if you understand church history and how God is *restoring* the church to its full potential, you would never believe that. God does not change. We cannot pick and choose what we want from God's Word, *we must eat the whole loaf of God's Bread if we want to grow up big and strong in Christ.*

Jesus Christ the *same yesterday, and to day, and for ever.*
Hebrews 13:8

In fact, it is sad to even think that. *What is the purpose of prophecy?* It is to ***encourage*** you to be all God wants you to be. Prophecy is the voice of God meeting you in a particular situation, encouraging you not to give up, encouraging you to hang in there, that God is with you.

But he that prophesieth speaketh unto men to *edification, and exhortation, and comfort.*

1 Corinthians 14:3

The devil knows that if we flow prophetically, encouraging one another, the *spirit of discouragement* will have no power. All saints should prophecy and encourage one another. The world is so quick to criticize and put you down. But as Christians, we should *not* be like the world.

In Graham Cook's book, *Developing Your Prophetic Gift*, he points out the difference between the role of the Prophet verses the gift of prophecy. Everyone who is saved and filled with the Holy Ghost should be encouraged to prophecy. Prophecy is not for oneself. It is not a selfish gift. Prophecy is always used to be a blessing to someone else.

Wherefore, brethren, *covet to prophesy,* **and forbid not to speak with tongues.**

1 Corinthians 14:39

If the gift of prophecy is used properly, God will send you to someone who is about to give up on God and you will *"exhort, edify, and comfort"* your brother or sister in the Lord. Your obedience to God and the use of the prophetic gift could mean the difference between life or death.

One of Satan's great weapons is discouragement, but God has a more powerful weapon; encouragement of his people, through the prophet and gift of prophecy. We cannot be deceived and fight against the prophetic Word of the Lord, but see it how God sees it, and use it for the *"edifying, exhorting, and comforting"* of the Body of Christ.

Barnabus..."The Son of Encouragement"

For he was a good man [Barnabus], and full of the Holy Ghost and of faith: and much people was added unto the Lord.

Acts 11:24

As we are changed from Glory to Glory, and as we are changed into the image of Jesus Christ, there is a man of God I want to be like, that exemplifies the nature of Christ. And that is Barnabas. The above scripture almost tells it all. *First*, he was a good man. A man that was respected by his enemies, as well as his friends. *Second*, he was filled with the Holy Ghost. He was empowered and ready to obey the will of God. And *thirdly*, because he was a good man and full of the Holy Ghost, many people were added to the Kingdom of God. I want to be like Barnabus. He was an encourager to the Body of Christ. He always saw the *"potential"* in people rather than their present condition.

The thief cometh not, but for to steal, and to kill, and to destroy: I am come that they might have life, and that they might have it more abundantly.

John 10:10

Satan is here to *"steal, kill and destroy."* Satan and his kingdom are here to assign *spirits of discouragement* to stop you from performing the will of God. God in his wisdom knows that we need help, so he sends Barnabus' into our life to encourage us. Jesus has come to bring us life and life more abundantly. Jesus wants us to be all we can be in Him. God has plans for us that we cannot even imagine. We serve a good God.

What does the name of Barnabus mean?

> **Joseph, a Levite from Cyprus, whom the apostles called Barnabas** [which means *Son of Encouragement*].
>
> **Acts 4:36 (NIV)**

Barnabas' name means *"the encourager."* He always sees the best in you and is patient to your weakness. That sounds like someone I know — Jesus. It is our aim to let God's character, through the Holy Spirit manifest through us. Barnabas let God's love flow through him.

What does it mean to encourage someone — *it means to give courage, hope, confidence, support, or help.* It also means to console or exhort. The Word says to love thy neighbor as thy self. Do you want to be comforted? Do you want someone to help you? We need to stop looking inward and start looking outward. God is looking for saints of God who will be his Barnabases in this day and hour. More than ever, the world needs a comforter, the world needs an encourager.

Being a minister's son, I have seen my dad, Dr. Joe Hester, (pastor of 30 years) get a burden in his heart for missions. He formed a non-profit company called *Missionary Encouragers, Inc.* based out of South Carolina.

The purpose of this organization is to *encourage* our missionaries who are overseas, helping them fulfill the work of the Great Commission.

> **And Jesus came and spake unto them, saying, All power is given unto me in heaven and in earth.**
>
> *Go ye therefore, and teach all nations,* **baptizing them in the name of the Father, and of the Son, and of the Holy Ghost:**
>
> **Teaching them to observe all things whatsoever I have commanded you: and, lo, I am with you alway,** *even unto the end of the world.* **Amen.**
>
> **Matthew 28:18-20**

God's command (not suggestion) is to go to the ends of the earth and preach the Gospel. As ministers and church leaders, we have to continue *encouraging* the Body of Christ to fulfill the call of God on our lives. We do not have to guess God's will concerning missions. *He says GO!* And keep on going until the job is finished. Sometimes it takes a group of believers who believe in the *principle of encouragement*...to help us finish the race that God has put before us. Praise God for organizations like *Missionary Encouragers, Inc.*, for the Body of Christ needs *encouragement* more than ever, if we ever expect to accomplish the command of Jesus called the *Great Commission*.

Barnabas was a prophet of God. He was a prophet with an apostolic anointing to go to the nations. He was a missionary as well. What was Barnabas' family history? He was a Levite. Remember, the Levite family used to perform the sacrificial offerings to God, as well as lead the singing in battle. Barnabas was a *"Praise Warrior!"* What do I mean by that? He always had a good attitude. When everyone was down in the mouth about the situation in their lives, Barnabas was there to say, "God will see you through this situation, keep your eyes on Jesus." He was a man of faith. He was a leader. He was a pioneer. He was an ambassador. He was a man that decided in his heart that even if no one would go with him in the work of the Lord, he would still go, even if it meant going alone. As Satan has launched out to attack the Body of Christ with the spirit of discouragement, God is raising up modern day Barnabas "son's of encouragers" to encourage his Church. Are you an encourager, or a discourager? Your positive or negative actions can determine success or failure for your life and the life of others.

David Encouraged Himself

And it came to pass, when David and his men were come to Ziklag on the third day, that the Amalekites had invaded the south, and Ziklag, and smitten Ziklag, and *burned it with fire;*

And had taken the women captives, that were therein: they slew not any, either great or small, but carried them away, and went on their way.

So David and his men came to the city, and, behold, it was burned with fire; and their wives, and their sons, and their daughters, were taken captives.

Then David and the people that were with him lifted up their *voice and wept,* until they had no more power to weep.

And David's two wives were taken captives, Ahinoam the Jezreelitess, and Abigail the wife of Nabal the Carmelite.

1 Samuel 30:1-5

Well things looked pretty bad for David and his men. The Amalikites had a surprise attack when David and his army were at another battle. It all seems so unfair. Have you ever been doing the work of the Lord, but Satan is allowed to attack you in a major way? It doesn't seem fair. Did David do something wrong? *No!* God wanted to see how David would *react* to this tragic situation. The pressure was mounting and the people wanted to kill him. *So what did David do?*

And David was greatly distressed; for the people spake of stoning him, because the soul of all the people was grieved, every man for his sons and for his daughters: *but David encouraged himself in the LORD his God.*

71

And David said to Abiathat the priest, Ahim-
elech's son, I pray thee, bring me hither the ephod.
And Abiathar brought thither the ephod to David.

And David inquired at the LORD, saying, Shall I
pursue after this troop? Shall I overtake them? And
he answered him, Pursue: for thou shalt surely overtake them, and without fail *recover all*.

1 Samuel 30:6-8

David encouraged himself in the Lord! As you
already have read in this chapter, I believe in the prophetic.
A prophetic word spoken out of an anointed man of
God, can mean the difference between life and death. I
believe in comforting one another, we need the Barnabus
spirit of encouragement more than ever in the Body of
Christ. We need to let the logos Word of God encourage
us. Just as David did, he encouraged himself.

And the prophet came to the king of Israel, and
said unto him, *Go, strengthen thyself,* and mark, and
see what thou doest: for at the return of the year the
king of Syria will come up against thee.

1 King 20:22

He did not call up a friend for prayer. He did not
run to the nearest conference to try to get a prophetic
word from God. David all alone, *encouraged* himself. I
believe David got alone with God and prayed. He sang
songs of praise to the Lord. He listened for the comforting words of the Lord, that said, all is going to be all
right. After David encouraged himself, I believe he was
strengthened and ready for war. Instead of self-pity, *a
by-product of the spirit of discouragement*, David encouraged himself. He asked the Lord, "can I get them back?"
God said: "Go for it, man of God!" David pursued his
enemy and he *recovered all*. What did I say? David
recovered all, not part of it, but *all*. Praise God! I heard

one minister put it this way; every time Satan would attack his ministry in a major way, he would write another book. Why are anointed books so important? Why is the devil afraid of books? Long after you die, you are still attacking Satan's kingdom!

In Exodus 22:7, it says, "that if a thief is found out he is to *re-pay double*." We all know that Satan is the master thief. When you find Satan is stealing from you, your family, your finances, your health, or your ministry, *DEMAND* that Satan pay you back *DOUBLE*. If he tries to steal your joy, demand double the joy back. If he steals $100 from you, demand in the name of Jesus, $200 back. If you do this one thing, Satan will stop his attack on you. There came a point in my life, that it really benefited me when Satan stole from me. I got double back. *What a deal!* But this is not *automatic*. I had to use God's Word and exercise my authority by faith as a child of the King. All things do work together for good to those that love the Lord (Romans 8:28). It is time to grow up. Sometimes God says, *"Encourage yourself in the Lord...it is up to you."*

Mark...Rescued By The Spirit of Encouragement

Was Paul different from Barnabas? Both were sent out from the church of Antioch (Acts 13:1). Both had hands laid on them and were sent out by the Holy Ghost. But there was also another man of God called *Mark*.

> **And Barnabas and Saul returned from Jerusalem, when they had fulfilled their ministry, and took with them John, whose surname was *Mark*.**
>
> **Acts 12:25**

Barnabas, Saul, and Mark were all sent off. But in the heat of ministry, Mark decided to turn back. He basically left when Paul and Barnabas, both needed him. He let them both down, as well as God. Now the journey was over. Mark had returned and Barnabas wanted Mark to go with them again. But Paul had other ideas. He did not want Mark to go with them. Mark was not trustworthy. When the going got tough, Mark would let them down again.

And some days after Paul said unto Barnabas, Let us go again and visit our brethren in every city where we have preached the word of the Lord, and see how they do.

And Barnabas determined to take with them John, whose surname was Mark.

But *Paul thought not good to take him* **with them, who departed from them from Pamphylia, and went not with them to the work.**

And the *contention was so sharp between them,* **that they departed asunder one from the other: and so** *Barnabas took Mark,* **and sailed unto Cyprus;**

And Paul chose Silas, and departed, being recommended by the brethren unto the grace of God.

And he went through Syria and Cilicia, confirming the churches.

Acts 15:36-41

So, what did Barnabas do? The *spirit of encouragement* rose up in him and he took young Mark under his wing. He told Paul that he wanted Mark to go with them again. Paul said, "No!" Their differences were so great that they split up, both going their separate ways. They were eventually reconciled later (1 Corinthians 9:6). When I first read this in the Word of God, I wondered who was wrong? This seemed like a real tragedy. But let us look a little deeper into what is happening here. Paul, who had an apostolic anointing, did not want a man around who could possibly leave him again when he was needed like on their last trip together. Therefore Paul was focused and did not want to be slowed down in any way. I call this a *pioneer anointing*, which we need more of in the Body of Christ. *But at the same time, we need Barnabases in the Body helping in the shepherding of the flock.* The *spirit of encouragement* must rise up and help us see the best in a person. We must be willing to forgive and receive them back, in love.

Love is very patient and kind, never jealous or envious, never boastful or proud,

never haughty or selfish or rude. Love does not demand its own way. It is not irritable or touchy. It does not hold grudges and will hardly even notice when others do it wrong.

It is never glad about injustice, but rejoices whenever truth wins out.

If you love someone, you will be loyal to him no matter what the cost. You will always believe in him, always expect the best of him, and always stand your ground in defending him.

1 Corinthians 13:4-7 (TLB)

What does it say? We will be loyal to him no matter what. No matter what! Barnabas took young Mark with him and Paul took Silas. But what was God up to? With their division, two teams now were spreading the Word of God. Thank God for the spirit of Barnabas. We need more than ever to console one another. We need more than ever to *encourage* one another. We need more than ever to exhort one another. I thank God everyday that he has not given up on me. So we must not give up on one another.

The *spirit of discouragement* has destroyed a lot of men and women of God. Satan loves to get you thinking about your circumstances rather than what God's Word says about them. Church, it is time to call forth the spirit of encouragement. The *spirit of encouragement* must be manifested for us to make it in these end times. We need Barnabases today more than ever. As we are looking at Satan's top ten list of ways to stop you, the spirit of discouragement is a powerful one. We have to know how to fight back, and shake ourselves loose from the enemy. We must study the Word, and stay connected to the local church. Like David, encourage yourself in the Lord. God is a good God. We need each other and when the spirit of discouragement hits, we must recognize it. We must fight to do the things we know to do; keep our eyes on Jesus in faith and not isolate ourselves from God, or the Body of Christ. *More that ever, the spirit of encouragement must be in us today, as we defeat the spirit of discouragement in our life.*

What is the next hurdle we must cross before we walk in our "calling?" *The spirit of diversion.*

Chapter 4
The Spirit of Diversion

I press toward the mark for the prize of the *high call-ing* of God in Christ Jesus.

Philippians 3:14

When all is said and done, *if I start and do not finish I do not get anything*. As Paul said in Philippians, he pressed toward the mark. In other words, he strained to reach the goal. He had a purpose in life and no one, or thing could *divert* him from the task that God had assigned to him. So many in the church today do not know what their calling is in life. They are going to church, but with no purpose. Saints are doing *"good"* things, but not the *"BEST"* things for God. If you do not know your purpose, you are an easy target for Satan and the *spirit of diversion*. If you do not know you have a purpose, Satan can keep you running in circles (wander-ing in the wilderness) and thus producing little fruit for the Kingdom of God.

Let us look at this fourth spirit, the *spirit of diversion* and see how Satan launches this spirit against the church and its leaders. Let us see how we can avoid being another victim. Let us see how we can keep our eyes on the target and obtain our prize, as we *Cross the Goal Line...Ten Yards at a Time*.

In Webster's Dictionary, the word *diversion* means *"to distract your attention"* and the word *distract* means *"to draw in another direction or confuse."* Simply put, the devil wants to get you off course. I have seen so many men and women of God start correctly after they realized the "call" on their lives, but in a short period of time get side-tracked. As the Holy Spirit is constantly drawing you to Himself, in the same way the devil is drawing the church out of the will of God. Satan is trying to get you to settle for less than what God has in His perfect will for your life.

> *O foolish Galatians, who hath bewitched you,* that ye should not obey the truth, before whose eyes Jesus Christ hath been evidently set forth, crucified among you?
>
> This only would I learn of you, Received ye the Spirit by the works of the law, or by the hearing of faith?
>
> Are ye so foolish? *having begun in the Spirit, are ye now made perfect by the flesh?*
>
> Galatians 3:1-3

Even if the church in Galatians had started off correctly, within a short period of time, the church had gotten off course. They were going the wrong way. They had missed the mark.

In the Church, once we are born-again, and we receive Jesus as our Lord and Savior, we should all seek the Lord on what we are "called" to do. I believe every Christian in the Body of Christ has a calling on his or her life. We are here on earth with a definite purpose and plan for our lives. Some of us realize our calling during the conversion experience, but many of us find out our calling later in our Christian walk. Once you realize what you are called to do, what next? I believe there are two distinct stages that we will experience after the call. I call the first stage the *standing stage*, or the preparatory stage. This is where God has called you, but now he *must train you for the work ahead* (Joshua 3:5). You are being set apart by God for a particular work that lies ahead of you. I call the second stage the *moving stage*, or the manifestation of your calling. You begin the work of the Lord. Both stages are very important. If you fail in any area in either of these two stages, you and your ministry could possibly fail to achieve the vision that God has given you. *Let us look at these two stages and see how they relate to one of Satan's weapons, the spirit of diversion.*

The Standing Stage

But they that wait upon the LORD shall renew their strength; they shall mount up with wings as eagles; they shall run, and not be weary; and they shall walk, and not faint.

Isaiah 40:31

I believe this is one of the hardest parts of your walk with the Lord. This is where most "die in the wilderness." I think one of the best books I have read on this subject was by a young minister, John Bevere, called, *The Voice of One Crying.* If you talk to any minister today, who is being used by God, they can tell you story after story of their *preparatory*, wilderness experience. It is fun, and challenging, as God is constantly stretching our faith.

How does the *spirit of diversion* relate to this stage of my ministry you may ask? *Very simply, the spirit of diversion tries to distract you so, you fail to prepare, you fail to be sanctified, you fail to be trained within your character, you fail to learn what you need to, you fail to know the intimacy of Jesus, and you fail to wait on the Lord.* It is my experience that your flesh hates this stage, it is not fun to your flesh. You are being *"crucified"* to self daily. When you die, *IT HURTS!* You are being crushed by the master so He can create from a lump of clay what He wants to make. I see so many saints "waiting" on God, doing nothing. In my seven year *standing stage*, I had to look at my life as if I were in school. **I was in the school of the Holy Spirit**. Even though seminary is good, *I felt my real training came from books I read, services I attended and ministers I served under*. This is the way God desired to train me.

In this stage of our ministry, *I believe getting started too soon is one of the biggest mistakes I've seen among ministers*. If God tells you to *go* and you do not, this is just as wrong. God wants us to combine wisdom and knowledge with zeal, to be released into our ministries. I asked the Lord: "why does it take so long?" He spoke to my heart: *"Son, I have a big ministry for you. Your fruit will be large and to handle the multitudes, your foundation must be just as large. You are my son, I love you, and I want you to be ready so you will not get hurt."* When He spoke these words into my heart, I knew that He was not holding me back because He was being mean, but because He had a ministry for me that was very special and He really loved me. **We do serve a good God!** Every time I think of getting ahead of God, I think of Jesus's ministry and how He prepared 30 years for a three and one half year ministry. I remind myself, if I step out of God's will and go without being *sent by God*, I am up for a big fall. If God is not behind me, I do not want to go. *How about you? IT IS WORTH THE WAIT.*

The Moving Stage

But be ye doers of the word, **and not hearers only, deceiving your own selves.**

James 1:22

Just as the *Standing Stage* is important to your calling by God, so is the *Moving Stage*. Remember, you are **called, prepared, and then sent.** I love the commercial on TV about Nike shoes. In the commercial where Bo Jackson (the famous Auburn running back) is training for an up coming football season, the commercial ends with the slogan *"JUST DO IT." Preparation time is so important, but don't get too comfortable in the wilderness.* What is the purpose for the wilderness? *It is to prepare you for war. It is to prepare you for ministry.* You are being formed into a warrior for God's army.

The Israelite people sought the comfort of the wilderness in Egypt, rather than occupy the promised land (which was war). How could this be? Like many of us today in the Christian faith, *we learn to just survive rather than live in victory.* We look for our comfort zone, but God is saying "Go take your land." We have established a "survival" mentality rather than a "warrior" mentality. What are we being prepared for? Simply, *YOU ARE BEING PREPARED FOR WAR!* We have to get an attitude toward the devil. These are my blessings from God and I want them back; enough is enough. I will not take it any longer, Devil. The *spirit of diversion* is such a powerful weapon of Satan because it is so subtle. We are in stage two, prepared to go to war, *but this spirit deceives us into believing the wilderness is all there is.* I left Egypt. I have freedom from the wilderness, but there is much more, the *Promised Land.* We have to be so careful to not just accept the good, when God has the *BEST* for us.

Call unto me, and I will answer thee, and *shew thee great and mighty things,* which thou knowest not.

Jeremiah 33:3

God has some great things in store for His Church... *GREAT AND MIGHTY THINGS.* Jesus has come to give us life and life more abundantly. As Christians, we have to reach our *"High Call"* in life. The *Spirit of Diversion* is used by the enemy so successfully. Why? *Because we get diverted by accepting less.* It is like we are at a fork in the road and we take the wrong fork. It is time that we ask ourselves, are we on the right fork in the road of life, or have we gotten "diverted" somewhere down the road?

The Spirit of Peace

How do we get back on course? **First**, we must realize we're off course, and going the wrong way. I heard one preacher say many people are very genuine in their belief, but still genuinely wrong. Being genuine is not a condition of being right. I remember a football game in high school where a defensive back intercepted the ball. He ran as hard as he could towards the goal line, he crossed the goal line, but the referee did not raise up his hands, because the player had run the wrong way. Millions upon millions have been deceived by Satan, thinking that they can go to heaven without the help of Jesus and the cross, seduced by the *spirit of diversion*. So, as Christians, how do we know when we have been diverted? *A sure way to discern is when we lose our peace.* What do I mean by that statement? Your inner knowing is *"checking"* you. Your inner man is saying: "something is wrong." My daily prayer is asking God, "Am I in your will?" If I do not get that "peace" back in my spirit, then I check myself and seek God until I find out what is wrong. In my ministry, people ask me: How do you know God's will? One way God directs us is through His *peace*.

> **Depart from evil, and do good;** *seek peace, and pursue it.*
>
> **Psalm 34:14**

> **But the fruit of the Spirit is love, joy,** *peace,* **long-suffering, gentleness, goodness, faith,**
>
> **Meekness, temperance: against such there is no law.**
>
> **Galatians 5:22,23**

Secondly, once we realize we are off course, *how do we get back on course?* We get back on course by asking God where we have missed it.

We must repent for missing it and ask God how to get back on course.

And Ahab told Jezebel all that Elijah had done, and withal how he had slain all the prophets with the sword.

Then Jezebel sent a messenger unto Elijah, saying, So let the gods do to me, and more also, if I make not thy life as the life of one of them by to morrow about this time.

And when he saw that, *he arose, and went for his life,* and came to Beersheba, which belongeth to Judah, and left his servant there.

But he himself went a day's journey into the wilderness, and came and sat down under a juniper tree: and he requested for himself that he might die; and said, It is enough; now, O LORD, take away my life; for I am not better than my fathers.

And as he lay and slept under a juniper tree, *behold, then an angel touched him,* and said unto him, Arise and eat.

And he looked, and, behold, there was a cake baken on the coals, and a cruse of water at his head. And he did eat and drink, and laid him down again.

And the angel of the LORD came again the second time, and touched him, and said, *Arise and eat; because the journey is too great for thee* [get back on track].

And he arose, and did eat and drink, and went in the strength of that meat forty days and forty nights unto Horeb the mount of God.

1 King 19:1-8

83

Elijah was near the brook. Elijah had fled from Jezebel, AND WAS OFF COURSE. God was trying to get him back on course. The water had dried up and food was running out. It was time to change his course or he would starve. *His peace was gone.* His stomach was empty. Elijah was off track, but in God's grace, he had a way to get Elijah back on track.

Thirdly, once you are back on track, God in his mercy, will *redeem and restore your time,* that you may be able to CROSS THE GOAL LINE.

> *Redeeming the time,* **because the days are evil.**
>
> **Wherefore be ye not unwise, but understanding what the will of the Lord is.**
>
> **Ephesians 5:16,17**

> **Walk in wisdom toward them that are without,** *redeeming the time.*
>
> **Colossians 4:5**

We must be heading in the right direction in order to score, and win the prize that God has for us. We cannot let the *spirit of diversion* get the best of us. We cannot let the *spirit of diversion* get us off track in the pursuit of the "HIGH CALLING" that God has for us. If we are *preparing* for ministry, or if we are in the full stage of our ministry, *we have to be aware and cautious of the spirit of diversion.* We have to be sensitive to the Holy Spirit and His *peace* in our life. We have to be guided by the "peace" of God (or lack there of) in our life. We cannot be running the wrong way, but in the right direction, *Crossing the Goal Line...Ten Yards at a Time.*

The next hurdle — *the spirit of distortion.*

Chapter 5
The Spirit of Distortion

They say that what is *right is wrong and what is wrong is right;* that black is white and white is black; bitter is sweet and sweet is bitter.

Woe to those who are wise and shrewd in their own eyes!

Isaiah 5:20,21 (TLB)

Besides Satan's schemes to destroy our thinking in the reality of who we are in Christ (identity), Satan can also *twist the truth* to make us believe what is really not truth. This spirit is called the *spirit of distortion.* One of the main problems with society today is, we are believing a lie, rather than the truth. We are sincere, but sincerely wrong. *Why is what we believe important?* Simply, our beliefs determine our behavior, and our behavior determines what we become. Our convictions determine our conduct, and our conduct determines our character.

The *spirit of distortion* can get us to think that our situation is hopeless when it is not. Things will never change. The situation becomes distorted into a bigger problem than it really is. This is a breeding ground for more fear. Your life becomes a breeding ground for more *distorted thinking.* It is so important to know God's word and to keep our eyes on JESUS. When we start listening to the devil, we can become immobilized.

Ever learning, and *never able* to come to the knowledge of the truth.

2 Timothy 3:7

Fear is Distorting the Truth

And when the servant of the man of God was risen early, and gone forth, behold, an host compassed the city both with horses and chariots. And his servant said unto him, Alas, my master! how shall we do?

And he answered, *Fear not: for they that be with us are more than they that be with them.*

And Elisha prayed, and said, LORD, I pray thee, *open his eyes,* that he may see. And the LORD opened the eyes of the young man; and he saw: and, behold, the mountain was full of horses and chariots of fire round about Elisha.

And when they came down to him, Elisha prayed unto the LORD, and said, Smite this people, I pray thee, with blindness. *And he smote them with blindness according to the word of Elisha.*

2 Kings 6:15-18

Elisha had to take the fear of man and cast it to the ground. He said, "open up your eyes." We have more on our side than the enemy. It is like playing a basketball game with five against one. Devil (1) and God (5). In fact, I will go on to say one thing further, God owns the team, the balls, the uniforms, etc., do you see my point? It sometimes *SEEMS* that Satan is bigger than God, ***BUT HE IS NOT...IT IS ONLY OUR THINKING THAT IS DISTORTED***. We are simply blinded to the truth. The devil is such a liar. I want to say, "He would want you to think that God has no power over him. He would want you to believe that God will never come through. He would want you to believe that he is stronger than God." Fear will rise up. The truth gets

86

distorted. You begin to believe a lie. Fear can cause the situation to get distorted. Fear can get you in left field, when you should be in right field.

Fear Can Immobilize You

For God hath not given us the spirit of fear; but of power, and of love, and of a sound mind.

2 Timothy 1:7

Why is the spirit of fear so immobilizing? Fear causes you to picture something *out of perspective.* The situation becomes *distorted.* The devil goes around seeking who he may devour. He roars, but he has no teeth. He tries to *intimidate* you. He looks tough, sounds tough, and walks like a bully, but just punch him in the nose, and he crumbles like a scared baby.

And there went out a champion out of the camp of the Philistines, named *Goliath,* of Gath, whose height was six cubits and a span.

And he had an helmet of brass upon his head, and he was armed with a coat of mail; and the weight of the coat was five thousand shekels of brass.

And he had greaves of brass upon his legs, and a target of brass between his shoulders.

And the staff of his spear was like a weaver's beam; and his spear's head weighed six hundred shekels of iron: and one bearing a shield went before him.

And he stood and cried unto the armies of Israel, and said unto them, Why are ye come out to set your battle in array? am not I a Philistine, and ye servants to Saul? choose you a man for you, and let him come down to me.

If he be able to fight with me, and to kill me, then will we be your servants: but if I prevail against him, and kill him, then shall ye be our servants, and serve us.

> **And the Philistine said,** *I defy the armies of Israel this day;* **give me a man, that we may fight together.**
>
> 1 Samuel 17:4-10

Even though Goliath was ten feet tall, if you hit him in the right place — he crumbles like any man. It is called the *spirit of intimidation.* Many times the devil will paralyze you with the spirit of fear through intimidation when in fact, "he is all talk and no action." I call it the bully on the playground syndrome, just call his bluff and he will run like a scared rabbit.

> **Submit yourselves therefore to God. Resist the devil, and** *he will flee from you.*
>
> James 4:7

Doctors Can Be Intimidating

Before my call into the ministry, I worked in the medical field and worked with many doctors. Many people are *intimidated by doctors* (including me), because they are well educated and many times live in a higher social stature. To be successful in this business field, you *cannot be intimidated* or you will not make it. Fear of man can be a real crippling factor in your business life (as well as ministry). I remember when I first started out after college, I had a doctor really embarrass me in a sales call. I could have given up and quit, but I got mad and studied even harder. I didn't allow fear to make me quit. I used to say to myself, this man puts on his pants one leg at a time, *just like I do. The way we perceive things (distortion), either right or wrong, can determine our success or failure in life.* We cannot let the spirit of fear or intimidation distort our correct picture of God and His plan for our life. We must have the *spirit of David* — knowing that our God is bigger than *ANYTHING THAT THE DEVIL CAN THROW AT US*. Let us all change our mentality, and start thinking like David and not reason like the fearful nation of Israel (Saul).

We Will Laugh At Satan

I will climb to the highest heavens and be like the Most High.

But instead, you will be brought down to the pit of hell, down to its lowest depths.

Everyone there will stare at you and ask, *"Can this be the one who shook the earth and the kingdoms of the world* [laugh]?

Can this be the one who destroyed the world and made it into a shambles, who demolished its greatest cities and had no mercy on his prisoners?"

Isaiah 14:14-17 (TLB)

This is one of my favorite scriptures. The world is gazing in the pit, observing Satan saying, "is this the guy who caused all the problems on the earth?" Ha Ha Ha! We perceive Satan to be so powerful, but remember, he still is a created being made by God. We sometimes give him too much credit. We need to be aware of his devices against us, but *WE CANNOT PERCEIVE HIM AS A FOE THAT CANNOT BE DEFEATED, FOR HE HAS ALREADY BEEN DEFEATED ON THE CROSS OF JESUS.* It is time for the Church to rise up, using our godly authority, putting Satan back in his place, *BEHIND US.* Praise God!

I was at a conference in North Carolina and heard a speaker use an acrostic on fear. F.E.A.R. — *Future Events Aren't Real!* How true! The *spirit of distortion* magnifies the enemy and makes him appear bigger than he really is. He makes your problem even larger than God in your eyes. Your problem is so big that even God himself cannot help you. As we worship and meditate on who God is, *IT IS TIME FOR US TO GET A RIGHT PICTURE OF WHO GOD IS, THE CREATOR OF THE WORLD, THE KING OF KINGS, THE LORD OF LORDS, THE ALPHA AND OMEGA, THE GREAT "I AM."* Simply, He is God.

Why does God hate the spirit of fear (sin) so much? When you are fearful you are saying that your God is not big enough to change the situation, you are not trusting your God. Fear has dispelled your faith. *The opposite of faith is fear.* In Numbers chapter 14, as Joshua and Caleb came back and gave a good report, the other ten spies spread a *bad report* to the people. Why did God react the way He did regarding the spies that gave a bad report? *God was angry that these men allowed the spirit of fear to take hold.* Instead of seeing that God is big enough to take on the giants of the land — the spies allowed fear to *intimidate* them into *settling for less and not the best* of God. In these last days, we are going to have to be warriors. The enemy is real, but at the same time he is not more powerful than God. His time is short. God has given to each individual a strategy to win land back from the devil. We cannot look and see the giants, but we must look and see that our God is more than a conqueror.

> *No weapon* that is formed against thee shall prosper; and every tongue that shall rise against thee in judgment thou shalt condemn. This is the heritage of the servants of the LORD, and their righteousness is of me, saith the LORD.
>
> Isaiah 54:17

> As it is written: "For your sake we face death all day long; we are considered as sheep to be slaughtered."
>
> No, in *all these things we are more than conquerors* through him who loved us.
>
> Romans 8:36,37 (NIV)

> I can do *all things through Christ* which strength-
> eneth me.
>
> Philippians 4:13

Our attitudes and thinking have to be *renewed* and
we have to start thinking like God and not like man. We
cannot let "talk shows" dictate our thinking. We cannot
let TV or radio dictate our thinking. We must let God's
Word dictate our thinking, trusting in Him to come
through in our situations. We have all authority, but we
have to *appropriate that authority* and take back what is
rightfully ours.

Awake...For the Time is Short

> Then shall the kingdom of heaven be likened unto
> *ten virgins,* which took their lamps, and went forth to
> meet the bridegroom.
>
> *And five of them were wise, and five were foolish.*
>
> They that were foolish took their lamps, and took
> *no oil with them:*
>
> But the wise took oil in their vessels with their
> lamps.
>
> *While the bridegroom tarried, they all slumbered
> and slept.*
>
> And at midnight there was a cry made, Behold, the
> bridegroom cometh; go ye out to meet him.
>
> Then all those virgins arose, and trimmed their
> lamps.
>
> *And the foolish said unto the wise,* Give us of your
> oil; for our lamps are gone out.
>
> Matthew 25:1-8

The *spirit of distortion* is a twisting spirit. It twists
your perspective of your authority in Christ. It twists
your perspective of the problem producing fear. *It dis-*

tracts the reality of the time to get the job done. Sometimes we feel that we have all the time in the world. As we look at the increasing evil in the world, we would agree that Jesus is returning again soon. No one knows the exact time, but God makes it very clear in His Word the attitudes we should have in regards to His second coming. WE MUST BE READY AT ALL TIMES...DOING HIS WILL. We cannot be like the foolish virgins...sleeping when they should be working, WE HAVE TO BE READY NOW.

> **For God says, "Your cry came to me at a favorable time, when the doors of welcome were wide open. I helped you on a day when salvation was being offered."** *Right now God is ready to welcome you.* **Today he is ready to save you.**
>
> **2 Corinthians 6:2 (TLB)**

Many times in our evangelistic effort we try to convince people that we do not know when we will die, that we might not have the opportunity to accept Jesus on our death bed. *But, in the same breath, we fail to have that same urgency in our own lives towards the Word of the Lord.* Would we live our lives differently if we knew that we only had a few days to live? Definitely, *yes!* In the same way, as children of the King, we have to live our lives *like each day could be the last one.*

> *In a moment, in the twinkling of an eye,* **at the last trump: for the trumpet shall sound, and the dead shall be raised incorruptible, and we shall be changed.**
>
> **1 Corinthians 15:52**

Could I have told my neighbor about the Lord? Did I tell my children that I love them today? Did I go to bed angry at my wife or husband? Did I forgive my friend? *Time is a precious commodity we cannot afford to take for granted.* Eternity is forever, but our time on earth is just for a season. We have to make everyday count for God, establishing His kingdom here on earth. We have to ask ourselves: "are my efforts today increasing the kingdom of God, or not?" The devil knows his time is short, we need to know it as well. We have to realize that we are living in the best times as Christians. We are about to take part with God in the biggest harvest of souls of all times. Remember, it says that Jesus cannot come back again until all Gentiles hear about the Gospel (Matthew 24:14). We are seeing it now as we are reaching the countries in the 10/40 window. The devil would like to distort you into thinking that you have all the time in the world. We took a trip to Argentina and the attitude of the land is "manana" which means *tomorrow the work gets done*. Tomorrow might never come. TODAY might be all you have. So, live for Jesus, walking in the light that God has given you for your life.

The *spirit of distortion* can cause you not to walk in the authority you have as a Christian. It can cause you to walk in fear, and it can cause you not to live with the sense of urgency you should walk in as a Christian. There is a big world out there, we have a lot to do in a short period of time. We can't be ignorant of how this spirit operates. Let us walk in our God given authority, walk in boldness, and make every day count for God. Let us keep moving forward and reach our goal! Let us not be diverted by falling into the temptation of the *spirit of distortion*.

The Twisting Spirit

According to Webster's dictionary, distortion means to misrepresent or to twist out of shape. When I was writing this chapter, the Lord put on my heart what this really means. This is a very damaging spirit and has crippled millions of Christians. This spirit has made them ineffective for the Lord. *When you twist something it becomes a completely different object.* Twisting the object can make it unusable for its intended purpose. For example, an arrow used in hunting is precisely made. Shot by the right marksman it can hit its target with complete accuracy. But at the same time, even Robin Hood could not hit the side of a barn with a twisted, warped arrow. Its original shape and function have been damaged. In fact, it does not even look like an arrow anymore. God intended for man to establish His kingdom here on earth. To go to the entire world making disciples, taking dominion over spiritual strongholds in cities, and nations. God has given us *all authority* in heaven and earth. We have a purpose and should aim straight and true at our target.

> Then he called his twelve disciples together, and gave them *power and authority* over all devils, and to cure diseases.
>
> and he sent them to preach the kingdom of God, and to heal the sick.
>
> Luke 9:1,2

> And spake unto him, saying, Tell us, by what *authority* doest thou these things? Or who is he that gave thee this authority?
>
> Luke 20:2

So what do I mean by the spirit of distortion? *What is Satan twisting?* Satan through his schemes has *twisted our image of ourselves,* how God sees us. He has twisted the truth of the saving power of Jesus.

Man's Self Image

The Christian has been given all authority over sickness and spiritual strongholds through the power of prayer. If we do not exercise our power and authority, it is like having a loaded gun, but never pulling the trigger.

When Jesus was in his ministry, the Pharisees kept asking: "by what authority are you doing these miracles?"

**For he taught them as one having *authority*, and
not as the scribes.**

Matthew 7:29

**And when he was come into the temple, the chief
priests and the elders of the people came unto him as
he was teaching, and said, *By what authority doest
thou these things?* And who gave thee this authority?**

Matthew 21:23

Satan questioned Jesus' authority right from the
very beginning. You must be grounded in knowing
your authority in Christ. Most Christians do not see
themselves as God sees them. Our thinking is distorted.
Our self image is twisted. Our authority in Christ is
weakened. God is waiting on us to establish His Kingdom. So why is the Body of Christ not doing its job? I
will list *four reasons*:

1. **Satan has twisted our view of who we are in
   Christ — our authority.**
2. **We fail to act on what we know.**
3. **The truth has been distorted.**
4. **We fail to realize the importance of hell.**

If Satan can keep us blinded in who we are in Christ
and keep us bound in guilt, he has us defeated. *This
book is all about speeding up your destiny in the things of God,
to get you back on track.* And if any revelation in this book
helps you move forward with God, then the purpose of
this book has been reached.

(1) Walking In Our Authority

It all starts at the cross. One has to understand
the foundation of one's faith. We are saved by grace

(Ephesians 2). We stand before God righteous if we are born again. Not because of our righteousness, but because of Jesus' righteousness on the cross. It is not us, but Jesus who said "I give you all authority." When Jesus left this earth, He said greater works will you do. Is that hard to believe? The miracle ministry of Jesus has been given to us.

Behold, *I give unto you* power to tread on serpents and scorpions, and over all the power of the enemy: and nothing shall by any means hurt you.

Luke 10:19

It is time for the Body of Christ to "walk in the authority" that God has given us. It is time to know who we are in Christ. It is time to change our image of who we think we are, *TO WHO GOD THINKS WE ARE.*

(2) We Fail To Act

Why do we need His authority? Our job is to establish His kingdom on earth. We are to be warriors for the Lord. Just as the infallibility of the Bible is important to the foundation of the Christian faith, so is the *authority* we must understand and act upon to be victorious and courageous for the Lord. God is all authority. We have His authority, BUT WE MUST USE IT FOR HIS GLORY.

Before the apostle Paul became a Christian, he tried to wipe out the church. After he met the Lord on the road to Damascus, he saw that God's authority was greater than his. He immediately fell to the floor and acknowledged Jesus as Lord. Paul had submitted to God. Paul had met God's authority. The church has to understand the authority it has now as believers and with *boldness come against the gates of hell.*

And I say also unto thee, That thou art Peter, and upon this rock I will build my church; and the *gates of hell shall not prevail against it.*

96

And I will give unto thee the *keys of the kingdom of heaven:* and whatsoever thou shalt bind on earth shall be bound in heaven: and whatsoever thou shalt loose on earth shall be loosed in heaven.

Matthew 16:18,19

(3) The Truth Has Been Distorted

When we are sensitive to the spirit, and the spirit is grieved by sin, we need to immediately check ourselves, ask for forgiveness, and move forward with the Holy Spirit. The human race has always tried to work their way to heaven by being "good enough." Almost every religion has either rejected what Jesus did on the cross, or added something to it.

For by grace are ye saved through faith; and that not of yourselves: it is the gift of God:

Not of works, *lest any man should boast.*

Ephesians 2:8,9

We have twisted the truth and accepted a lie. The world has bought religion, but not Jesus. *Sin can distort the truth.* Sin has a way of making you feel naked to who you are in Christ. Satan wants you to feel guilty, not pray, feel condemnation and ultimately run from God. Sin basically makes you forget the forgiveness power of God.

When the woman saw that the fruit of the tree was good for food and pleasing to the eye, and also desirable for gaining wisdom, she took some and ate it. She also gave some to her husband, who was with her, and he ate it.

Then the eyes of both of them were opened, and they realized they were naked; so they sewed fig leaves together and made coverings for themselves.

97

Then the man and his wife heard the sound of the LORD God as he was walking in the garden in the cool of the day, and they hid from the LORD God among the trees of the garden.

But the LORD God called to the man, "Where are you?"

He answered, "I heard you in the garden, and *I was afraid because I was naked; so I hid.*"

And he said, "Who told you that you were naked? Have you eaten from the tree that I commanded you not to eat from?"

Genesis 3:6-11 (NIV)

Sin is definitely offensive to Jesus. It is the very works that He was made manifest to destroy. In First John it says, "we must deal with sin at the cross." But we have to quickly see ourselves once again forgiven and come boldly to the cross of Jesus. God does not see us condemned, but redeemed. Praise God! God wants us to be both *"humble and bold"* as we approach Him. *Humble* knowing who God is, but *bold* knowing who we are as the children of the King, we are His sons and daughters. As an heir to the throne, as a child of the King, we can expect God to fellowship with us.

Let us therefore come *boldly unto the throne of grace,* that we may obtain mercy, and find grace to help in time of need.

Hebrews 4:16

For which I am an ambassador in bonds: that therein I may *speak boldly,* as I ought to speak.

Ephesians 6:20

You have to see yourself as God sees you; not how you see yourself, or the accuser of the brethren, Satan, sees you. *You cannot let the spirit of distortion twist your view of how God sees you.* Satan wants to take away our boldness. He wants to keep us silent, and not pray. WE HAVE TO SEE OURSELVES AS GOD SEES US, COVERED WITH THE BLOOD OF JESUS.

(4) Hell Is Real

Submitting to authority is one of the toughest things to do at times. Satan fell from grace because he could not submit. He was full of pride and rebellion. Because of his sin of rebellion, he was placed in hell. If we do not know Jesus (dealing with our sin of rebellion) then, like Satan, we can join him as well. It is tragic enough to be slowed down in the destiny for our lives, *but to never find God or not reach heaven is a catastrophe.*

As a church, if we believe deep in our hearts, that Jesus is the *only way* to get to heaven and HELL IS REAL, we would be doing everything in our power to make sure that the world knows about Jesus. This alone should be our motivation. What is the problem? One of the problems is that the world and the church do not believe that hell is real. The devil is only make believe, "a man on TV dressed up in a red outfit." Hell is real and so is the devil. Once we get a revelation of that, we will start to see people the way God sees them, *lost without Jesus in their hearts.*

The Lord is not slow in keeping his promise, as some understand slowness. He is patient with you, *not wanting anyone to perish,* **but everyone to come to repentance.**
2 Peter 3:9 (NIV)

I was thinking, anyone who would not receive Jesus as Lord and not go to heaven had to be literally crazy. Who, in their right mind, would want to go to hell? So why has mankind, in massive numbers, turned from God? We are blinded!

In whom the god of this world hath *blinded the minds* **of them which believe not, lest the light of the glorious gospel of Christ, who is the image of God, should shine unto them.**

2 Corinthians 4:4

We have all heard that the truth shall set you free. Well, Satan has blinded their eyes so they cannot see the truth. The road is narrow and many will not get there. Satan has twisted the spiritual eyes of many to the grace of God, and the debt that Christ paid for in full on the cross.

Satan is the accuser of the brethren, a liar and deceiver. He can *distort* the way you perceive yourself. He makes you think as though you were not bought with a price, but God sees us behind the veil of Christ. The spirit of *distortion* can blind you toward the Gospel and the love of God. Are you distorted in your self image? Do you know who you are in Christ? Are you working for God's love or *are you receiving his love by grace*? Are you allowing the *spirit of distortion* to slow you down in God's "calling" on your life? *Let us move forward with God, moving ten yards farther as we have victory over the spirit of distortion.*

*The next step — **the spirit of disobedience**.*

Chapter 6
The Spirit of Disobedience

But of the fruit of the tree which is in the midst of the garden, God hath said, Ye shall not eat of it, neither shall ye touch it, lest ye die.

And the serpent said unto the woman, *Ye shall not surely die.*

Genesis 3:3,4

Satan successfully provided an environment of doubt in the mind of Eve. He said, "you shall not surely die." Which we know was a lie. Satan is the author of lies. Eve ate the fruit of the tree anyway and thus, lost her position in the Garden of Eden. And because of her *disobedience*, it also affected her husband. They both had to leave their home, because the lust of the flesh and the *spirit of disobedience* were allowed to operate in their lives.

Why is the *spirit of disobedience* such a powerful weapon used by Satan? Because it causes you to doubt the very one that loves you the most — God. So many times, in our finite minds, we think we are smarter than God. We think we have all the answers. But God says in His Word that He will take the foolish things of the world to confound the wise (1 Corinthians 1:27). We do not know the beginning from the end. The only one who knows the future and the reason behind these actions and plans is God Himself. I once heard a pastor ask, "what is one of the biggest problems of the Christian world today?" He replied, that 90 percent of all Christians are confused. *Why?* Because we try to figure out the answer to everything.

> **Trust in the LORD with all thine heart; and *lean not unto thine own understanding.***
>
> **Proverbs 3:5**

What happened to living by faith? Many times God does not reveal the whole picture to us. We might only know a piece of the puzzle. I can just imagine God telling Moses the whole story in advance. "Moses you are going to call down plague after plague, the first born child of the Egyptians will be killed, and you are going to part the Red Sea and take more than a million people into the wilderness." Moses probably would have fainted and stayed longer on the back side of the desert.

God many times told people to do things that did not make sense. If we asked our church members today to do some of things that Jesus did, we might get locked up in a mental hospital. For example, Jesus spit in his hands, made mud, and put it in a man's eye. Can you imagine doing that in a service today? Jesus told an important ruler to go dip himself in the muddiest water of the area seven times. Why not just go dip one time in a local pond that was clean? It did not make a lot of sense. But what did the man do? He did not try to reason. Why did he do what Jesus said? He acted upon the Word of God and was healed. Simply, obedience produced his miracle and disobedience would have produced disappointment. The blind man didn't stop Jesus from putting mud in his eye. He let Jesus do something that did not make sense to him in the natural. He trusted God, acting upon His Word, not reasoning with his natural mind.

The *spirit of disobedience* worked in Eve's life, because she started reasoning in her human mind, when in fact, she did not know the entire story. When Adam and Eve were forced out of the Garden of Eden, Satan now had legal ground because of their sin. Thus, opening up the entire human race to be influenced by the *spirit of disobedience* and rebellion. The spirit of rebellion works hand in hand with the spirit of disobedience.

> *For the good that I would I do not: but the evil which I would not, that I do.*
>
> Now if I do that I would not, it is no more I that do it, but sin that dwelleth in me.
>
> I find then a law, that, when I would do good, evil is present with me.
>
> **Romans 7:19-21**

We are born with a sin nature. We do the very things we do not want to do.

A good example of this is found in our children. Anyone who has ever had children will agree with this statement, "I do not have to teach my children to be selfish or rebellious, it just comes naturally." With the fall of Adam and Eve, we now have this inherited sin — called the *spirit of rebellion*.

The Non-Submissive Pastor

Remember, this book is to help the minister of God finish the race and cross the goal line. As ministers of the gospel, the *spirit of rebellion* can cause real problems in a church, if not dealt with. According to Webster's dictionary, rebellion, "is open, bold resistance to authority." Who is the authority in the church? The Pastor. I have heard sermon after sermon on the church being submitted to the house and the pastor. *Now what about the pastor*? Who are you submitted to? My other book,

Finishing The Job: A New Look at an Old Command, goes into depth on this subject. Pastors today are not submitting to prayer. Pastors are not being accountable to other pastors. Flocks are being raped and not properly shepherded. God says He will give us shepherds after his own heart. Today, we have many churches with pastors who tell their congregation to submit to their authority, but they will not submit to anyone. God, in His proper order, has everyone reporting to somebody. Who are you accountable to? I hear all the time, "I only report to God." How can you be submitted to God and not submit to any man? I am not saying to obey man when it is contrary to the Word of God, but we all have to find our accountability partner.

My dad was a Lieutenant Colonel in the Air Force. He was a fighter pilot. I was born on an air force base in Hampton, Virginia. I remember as a young boy watching the soldiers march hour after hour doing the same drills over and over. I would ask myself — why so much marching? Why so much routine drilling? I asked my dad and I will always remember his words: "It teaches the combat ready soldier the two most important things needed in a wartime state; *obedience and discipline.*" The military understands the importance of obeying instructions and self discipline (self government). The ability to follow an order can mean the difference between life and death, not only for yourself, but your actions could make the difference for your troops as well. Today, more than ever, we cannot break rank. We must follow our leaders, assuming our positions in God's army.

> **They shall run like mighty men; they shall climb the wall like men of war; and they shall march every one on his ways, and *they shall not break their ranks.***
> **Joel 2:7**

We need an obedient spirit back in the church again, but more than that, we need an obedient, submissive spirit for pastors. I am so excited to be a part of God's movement of "Promise Keepers." The goal of the ministry is to restore the man back to his rightful authority, in the home, the community, and the church. The role of the father has to re-establish itself. We all know the importance of the role of the father in one's individual family. But what about the church? What about the family of churches? Pastors need pastors. Pastors also need fathers.

> **And he shall turn the *heart of the fathers to the children, and the heart of the children to their fathers*, lest I come and smite the earth with a curse.**
>
> **Malachi 4:6**

To win the world and fulfill the Great Commission, God must establish the father's heart back into the leaders of God's churches. More than ever, we need pastors who can be "father's" to other pastors. We all need the "father's spirit" loosed back into the church today. The work of the Lord will be quickened with the Father's guidance rather than starting fresh each time a ministry is started, or a church is planted. The Father of souls will provide the pastor proper covering, thus, speeding up the work of the Lord. God's way is always best.

Spirit of Obedience

> *If ye be willing and obedient, ye shall eat the good of the land:*
>
> *But if ye refuse and rebel,* ye shall be devoured with the sword: for the mouth of the LORD hath spoken it.
>
> **Isaiah 1:19,20**

The spirit of disobedience can cause you to doubt. It can cause you to rebel and not submit. It can slow down the work of the Lord. The spirit of obedience can cause you to be blessed. I do not know about you but, I would rather be blessed, than cursed.

What spirit in King David was such an important quality in this man of God? Why did God call David "A man after his own heart?" (1 Samuel 13:14). It was the *spirit of obedience* that worked strong in his life (Acts 13:22). Before we look at David, let us first look at King Saul and find out why God rejected him.

> **And the LORD said unto Samuel,** *How long wilt thou mourn for Saul,* **seeing I have rejected him from reigning over Israel? fill thine horn with oil, and go, I will send thee to Jesse the Bethlehemite: for I have provided me a king among his sons.**
>
> **1 Samuel 16:1**

This is a tragic story. Samuel was a prophet of God who wanted Saul to succeed. He was a man of compassion. He charged Saul to obey the Word of the Lord (1 Samuel 12:14,15). But what happened to cause King Saul to lose his position as king? *Saul was disobedient not just once, but twice. First*, Saul did not wait on the Lord (1 Samuel 10). Right from the start of his reign the spirit of disobedience ruled in his life. *Secondly,* he did not obey by not killing all the enemies (1 Samuel 15:3). This was the last straw (1 Samuel 13:13,14). Samuel called Saul a fool. Saul's disobedience now had cost him the kingdom. What caused Saul to disobey God? Sometimes, we think he did a horrible act like murdering someone, or ran away in battle. In fact, it was none of these. Let us look at the subtle way the spirit of disobedience worked in Saul's life.

First, he did not wait long enough (1 Samuel 10). How many times have we been guilty of getting ahead of God? How many times have we been impatient with

God? Let us not be so quick to judge Saul. *Secondly*, Saul did not obey the command of God totally. What did Saul do wrong? As Saul went into battle he was to destroy *all* the Amalekites, even the king. Saul thought he had a great victory. It seemed from man's point of view, he was successful, but in God's view he had been defeated (1 Samuel 15: 20-24).

How many times have we walked only a half mile when God said to walk a mile? What if the ruler that dipped himself in the Jordan river only dipped six times, and not seven? (2 Kings 5:10-15). What if the Israelite people only walked around the walls of Jericho five times, rather than seven? (Joshua 6;24:11). The ruler would not have been healed and the walls of Jericho would not have fallen. As ministers, many times we obey God in some areas in our life, *but will not surrender all areas of our lives to Him*. God is not looking for partial obedience, but *total obedience*. We all want more anointing and more of God's power. Is God waiting on you? Are all areas of your life surrendered to Him? Jesus does not want part of your life, but all of it. God does not want partial surrender, but total surrender. Saul lost his anointing. Saul lost his kingdom. Thank God for his grace today, by the sacrifice of his son, JESUS. Let us be quick to ask God to forgive us when we have missed it. Let us not be a Saul, but follow the pattern of David.

David — A Man of Obedience

Why was David called a friend of God? Why was David so anointed and successful in his life? David murdered a man and committed adultery. In man's eyes, these sins were worse than what King Saul did. Saul's only fault was that he did not wait one day and failed to kill all, after a great victory in battle. David was a murderer and adulterer. So, what was the difference? *David had an obedient spirit.* He was quick to repent and even quicker to obey.

> **And Samuel said, Hath the LORD as great delight in burnt offerings and sacrifices, as in obeying the voice of the LORD? Behold, to *obey is better than sacrifice,* and to hearken than the fat of rams.**
>
> **1 Samuel 15:22**

As we discussed earlier in this chapter, rebellion is a serious sin. God does not take it lightly. In First Samuel 15:23, rebellion is compared to the sin of witchcraft. He also calls stubbornness as iniquity and idolatry. In the old testament, the sin of witchcraft and idolatry were worthy of death (Exodus 22:12, Leviticus 20:6, Deuteronomy 13:12, Micah 5:10). Since Saul became both rebellious and stubborn, it is little wonder why God finally rejected him as king. God did not reject Saul as a person, but took away his position as the leader of the nation. We all make mistakes, but like David, we must be quick to repent and quick to obey. Let us not be put on the "bench" by God for our disobedience.

God expects more from you as leaders. To whom much is given, much is required. What you could get away with when you had a small ministry, now God is saying no more. He's judging the House of the Lord first, before the rest of the land. And God judges His leaders first. Let us all take a personal examination of our own lives.

> **Examine yourselves to see whether you are in the faith; test yourselves. Do you not realize that Christ Jesus is in you — unless, of course, you fail the test?**
>
> **2 Corinthians 13:5 (NIV)**

Are you being completely obedient in what God called you to do? Are you fulfilling your role in the Body of Christ in what He has for you? Let us be honest with ourselves, we have all missed it at times. God really wants to bless us, our families, and ministries, but we have to have a heart like David, an *obedient spirit*. The *spirit of disobedience* is a weapon launched not just against the preacher and ministers of the Gospel today, but all the church as a whole. We have to recognize this spirit as witchcraft and stop it, before it stops us. *We have to stop settling for the good, and achieve God's best, by walking in the spirit of obedience.* Now, it is time to cross the next hurdle — the spirit of division.

Chapter 7
The Spirit of Division

Can two walk together, *except they be agreed?*

Amos 3:3

One of our biggest jobs in this last hour is to take the Gospel to the entire earth. This is a big job for the *whole* Body of Christ. Not just the pastor, not just the missionaries, but *ALL*. If everyone does their part as one mobilized army, the job will get done. *Satan knows if we come together this way, he will not have a chance against God's people.* This is why Satan uses the *spirit of division* against the Body of Christ in such a powerful way. Let us look at the spirit of division and find out what Satan knows that we don't. Let us see how Satan uses this spirit against us in: (1) the church, (2) marriages, and (3) leadership — the pastor. Let us look at what we can do to fight back and win against the *spirit of division* in our lives. But first let us define what the *spirit of division* is.

According to Webster's dictionary, division is *"anything that divides"* or *"cause to disgrace."* The spirit of division is anything that causes two people, two groups, or two nations to not agree. When JESUS was accused by the religious leaders of His day of being Satan, He replied "A divided kingdom ends in ruin, a city or home divided against itself cannot stand" (Mark 12:25). Jesus knew perfectly well that our strength depends on working together rather than against one another. As I heard one speaker put it, "T.E.A.M. means Together Everyone Accomplishes More." *How true!*

(1) Satan Divides The Church

What does Satan know that the Church does not know? Satan knows the *power* that will transpire in the heavenlies if the Body of Christ starts coming together for a *single purpose*. One of the greatest weapons as Christians is prayer. When we pray to God, individually we gain power, but what happens when an entire church, city, or nation prays together? It is called the *corporate prayer*. *Simply, there is more power in numbers.*

And five of you shall chase an hundred, and an hundred of you shall put ten thousand to flight: and your enemies shall fall before you by the sword.

Leviticus 26:8

As Satan is Lord of this earth, it is our duty to enforce God's will on this earth through prayer. Simply, we have more impact in the spirit realm when "two or more" agree on a matter. The battle is in the heavenlies against principalities in high places (Ephesians 6:12). The church has more power with more people praying. I am so excited to be a part of praying through the *10/40 Window* with many others like Cindy Jacobs and Peter Wagner. These two generals in God's army are making such a super effort in unifying Christians for prayer. They learned long ago it takes more than themselves to get the job done. With the technology of the TV, satellite, airplanes and computers (Internet), we can mobilize a great army today. God is moving upon His people to pray, as we focus on a single purpose, fulfilling the Great Commission. Satan knows and fears the Church when the Church gets united. That is why He fights so hard to keep us *divided*.

(2) Satan Divides Marriages

Satan tries to divide us within our own families. As a minister, I realize my first ministry is unto God. My second ministry is unto my family, and my third is to my church. In many ministries, we have seen this order reversed. We have seen pastors in love with their church and not their wife.

> **Husbands, *love your wives,* even as Christ also loved the church, and gave himself for it.**
>
> **Ephesians 5:25**

How can we unite a city for the Lord, when we cannot keep a marriage unified? *We are out of order.* We have all seen great ministries fall because the marriage institution was destroyed. It would be sad to say: "I saved the world, but lost my own family."

What aspect of marriage makes it a point of attack for Satan? It involves our sexual character. Infidelity in marriage is a major problem today in society, and as well in Christian homes. Sexual sin is the only sin that can involve the creation of another soul. This sin can directly affect another person's life, and indirectly it can affect many lives. The devil plays on a God-given physical drive to be wed in the marriage bed and orchestrates events to put you into a position where he can push your button. If you yield when he pushes your button, he has knocked you out. Your sexual character must be yielded to the Holy Spirit.

Your marriage must be top priority, **NOT YOUR MIN- ISTRY.** God has made you a team. God looks at you as *one flesh,* we have to look at ourselves in the same way. We must keep the lines of communication open at all times. If a problem arises, go to your spouse and then, both of you go to God. Work it out together. *Staying in agreement* leaves no room for the spirit of strife and contention to enter. Don't be another victim, but keep your team strong. My wife and I facilitate a marriage course called, "His Needs, Her Needs" from Family Dynamics, Inc. twice a year. If you desire to strengthen your marriage, you might consider joining us in one of our eight-week sessions taught throughout the United States.

(3) Satan Divides The Leaders — The Pastors

> And I will give *you pastors according to mine heart,* which shall feed you with knowledge and understanding.
>
> **Jeremiah 3:15**

God did not say pastors after *their* own hearts, but after *His heart.* Pastors seeking to build their own individual kingdoms rather than the Kingdom of God, will not succeed. The Bible says that they will know that we are Christians by our love for one another (1 John 4:12). As leaders, we have failed in this area. How do we expect members of our church to get together when pastors in a city cannot even get together to pray for their own city? *Something is wrong.* Paul and Barnabas had the same problem in their time. It says, "but the people of the city were divided in their opinion about them" (Acts 14:14). *I am not promoting unity for the sake of unity.* But if another preacher is preaching the Gospel message that you are saved by accepting JESUS and asking forgiveness for sin, *we should be able to pray and worship together. Jesus should be our common element of union,* not our doctrine or denominational differences. If our leaders are divided, then so are our churches. How does the world know that we are Christians? *By our love. By our unity. We have to learn that most simple lesson.* We are only

114

walking in a fraction of the power that God wants us to have. It is God's desire to give us more, but we (the Church) are limiting God by being divided. Why can't we win our city for the Lord? Why can't we move in power as a Body of Christ in our nation? *We haven't learned how to come together.* Satan knows what will happen if we come together, it is called "the world coming to Christ." He is fighting us with all fury to divide our troops. What are some of the ways that Satan divides leaders of our churches? What are some of the ways that Satan divides the pastors of a city?

A) *Spirit of Individualism*

Some of us have our own agendas. We are more concerned about our own plan rather than the overall plan of God. Satan was kicked out of heaven because he wanted to start his own church rather than be a part of the big church. I am not saying that it is wrong to go and begin a new ministry. But what I am saying is, we all have a plan and purpose ordained by God. *We have to be in the proper order.* In our ministry, we have traveled all over the world, but American pastors do not want to submit to anyone. We are not accountable to anyone. We have churches all over America with 50 members or less who have been that way for years. Maybe God wanted to use them as a *servant* in a larger church, but because of their rebellious, prideful, and *individualistic spirits* they stay in that dead place and live on the backside of the desert. It is time to break this spirit that divides — the spirit of individualism.

B) *The Spirit of Competition*

There is nothing wrong with goal setting. But when this spirit sets us against one another rather than working together toward the same goal — reaching the world for JESUS — something is wrong. Before I entered the ministry, I worked for Dupont in their medical division. In our marketing meetings, we were constantly trying to find a way to outdo our competitor. Competition is good as long as it helps achieve excellence in individuals and in business. When competition makes us fight for territory in a community (*territory preservation*) and we start accusing other pastors of "stealing our flock," this is wrong. There are enough "lost people", quit getting all upset about the flock that left. Maybe, because of your wrong "attitude," they should have left. It is time to get our *focus* back on the "lost sheep." It is time to get our "hearts" right with God. Another church is not our competition, but our TEAM MATE. Let us all re-think how our church fits into the big picture — *THE CHURCH AS A WHOLE.*

We travel around the world and see the billions of people who have never heard the Gospel even one time. It makes me so mad, to think pastors are fighting over a few sheep in an area when the world is going to hell. The spirit of God is so grieved at our petty bickering and squabbling.

The *spirit of competition* not only causes us to fight among ourselves, but sometimes in our competitiveness, we compare ourselves to the next pastor down the street. We have a nice congregation, we have a nice building, we get complacent. We get satisfied. But, God has called us to reach the world, He has called us to do more. The only person we can compare ourselves to is JESUS. Jesus is our example. The *spirit of competition* is only good when our enemy is Satan, not one another. The world is our field of ministry, all we have to do is ask for the nations (Psalm 2:8). Let us quit fighting over the same turf, *BUT START FIGHTING THE DEVIL FOR THE LOST AND DYING WORLD WHO DOES NOT KNOW JESUS.*

C) *The Spirit of Offense*

Then said he unto the disciples, It is impossible
but that offenses will come: **but woe unto him, through**
whom they come!
Luke 17:1

It is not *if* offense will come, *but when*. And when
offense comes, *HOW WILL YOU REACT?* In fact, it
takes the power of God to *not* be offended. I believe that
Satan has the most success with the spirit of offense to divide
the Body of Christ than any of the spirits.

What was Jesus' answer? We are to love our enemies. Many times the one who offends is the one closest
to you, a family member, Christian leader, or another
Christian friend. Jesus says to love your enemy (Matthew
5:44-47). It takes the *power of God* to walk in that type of
love (Agape).

In our ministry, we have so many people who have
been hurt by a loved one, business partner, or another
church leader. The spirit of rejection and wounded spirit
rest upon that individual. Until we deal with these
issues, it is almost impossible to go any further! *Why?*

A brother offended is harder to be won than a strong
city: **and their contentions are like the bars of a castle.**
Proverbs 18:19

He or she has a wall of protection up. You have to deal
with this offended spirit first. We all have this self protection mechanism within us. But if we do not receive our
healing, we will never have the intimate relationship we
should have with our family, spouse, pastor, or our God.
We will be unable to receive the *fullness* of God's love.

One of the classic examples of being offended is the
story of David and Saul (1 Samuel 16-31). Many times,
Saul hated David for no reason. The spirit of jealousy

rose up in King Saul. What is important here is not that Saul was trying to kill David, *but how did David react?* Instead of hating Saul, David would not lay a hand on God's chosen king.

And David said to Abishai, Destroy him not: for *who can stretch forth his hand against the LORD's anointed, and be guiltless?*

David said furthermore, As the LORD liveth, the LORD shall smite him; or his day shall come to die; or he shall descend into battle, and perish.

The LORD forbid that I should stretch forth mine hand against the LORD's anointed: **but, I pray thee, take thou now the spear that is at his bolster, and the cruse of water, and let us go.**

1 Samuel 26:9-11

Saul has to answer to God, it is not David's place to hurt Saul. Vengeance is the Lord's — not David's. David had to *forgive* Saul and *respond* correctly. We have to lay down our rights. We have to walk in humbleness and not pride. We have to think of others more highly than ourselves. We have to walk in a *spirit of forgiveness* and not in a *spirit of offense*.

If we are going to receive anything from God, we cannot fall into the *trap* of *offense*. One of the best books I have read on the subject of offense is called, *The Bait of Satan* by John Bevere. John goes into detail how Satan has used the "bait of offense" to ensnare many Christians. The *spirit of offense* is still a very powerful weapon that Satan uses to slow down and defeat the Body of Christ. We have to be aware of the schemes of the devil, having victory over the *spirit of offense*. David could have sought revenge and fallen into Satan's trap, *but he did not.* How about you? Have you fallen prey to Satan's trap of offense? Are you harboring a grudge against someone?

Let us all walk in the spirit of forgiveness and the love of God. *Let us not fall prey to the trap of offense.*

D) *The Spirit of Denominationalism*

Coming from a large denominational church, I will be the first one to say I love my church, *but when one denomination puts down another denomination and thinks they are the only church that is right — then, that is not God.* That is called the *spirit of pride.* If a church believes that Jesus is the answer and believes in the same Gospel as the Bible; then we are in the same Body of Christ. Yes, there are differences in worship style, but if you are born again — we should love each other; remember, we are all saved by *grace.* We were all sinners before we found Jesus (Romans 3:9,10).

The disciples came up to Jesus and said there is a group that is casting out devils in Your Name. What did Jesus say? "If they are *not* against you, then they are for you" (Mark 9:38-40). We have to start looking at the Church as the Church of Jesus Christ (as a whole) rather than Baptist, Methodist, Assembly of God, etc. We have to start seeing the Church like God sees it, as ONE CHURCH — HIS CHURCH. We have to start discarding man- made labels and start picking up God's vision of His Church, as *ONE LORD, ONE FAITH, AND ONE BAPTISM.*

Endeavouring to keep the unity of the Spirit in the bond of peace.

There is one body, and one Spirit, even as ye are called in one hope of your calling;

One Lord, one faith, one baptism,

One God and Father of all, who is above all, and through all, and in you all.

Ephesians 4:3-6

E) The Spirit of Racism

What then? *are we better than they? No,* in no wise: for we have before proved both Jews and Gentiles, that they are all under sin.

Romans 3:9

One of the biggest problems Paul had in his times were *ethnic differences*. The Jews thought they were better than the Gentiles. The Jews thought the Gentiles were dogs. Paul stated that no one group of people is better than the other. All are sinners before coming to the saving knowledge of Jesus Christ (Romans 3:9,10). I was listening to Peter Wagner, director of the World Prayer Center in Colorado Springs, Colorado, on TV and he was asked what he thought the prevailing spirit was operating over Chicago. Mr. Wagner replied, "I do not know what is operating in Chicago, but the spirit that the nation has to deal with is: *the spirit of racism*." In Chicago, if you describe a Christian church, you either describe it as an Evangelistic or Pentecostal church and then you describe it either as a white church, or a black church.

We have to start looking at the Church like Jesus does — on this rock I will build my Church (Matthew 16:18). ***ONE CHURCH!*** He was not talking about a Roman Catholic church, Baptist church, Assembly of God church, Black church or White church. He was talking about *"The Church,"* not even the American Church, **but the World Church**. Our view of the Church has to change. The selfish attitude that, "my church is the best and the only church that is in the will of God" is a lie from hell. It takes effort on our part to change. The Church must move in God's direction, we must move into seeing the Church as *One*. We must start loving our brother as our neighbor. We must start unifying to accomplish His purposes. We must start "walking in agreement," *then His power will be released on His Church.*

The *spirit of division* is a powerful spirit that Satan has launched against the Church. He has attacked our churches in our cities, our marriages, and even the leaders, our church pastors. What do we need more than ever in the Body of Christ, we need to walk in the "*spirit of reconciliation.*"

The Spirit of Reconciliation

And all things are of God, who hath reconciled us to himself by Jesus Christ, and hath given to us the *ministry of reconciliation.*
2 Corinthians 5:18

We know that offense will come. We know that it is our response that God is concerned with. So, what should our response be? What is the spirit of reconciliation?

We must *first* walk in a spirit of forgiveness. It is the will of God that we forgive. What are the consequences of refusing to let go of offense? God will not forgive you. That is pretty serious (Luke 6:37, Matthew 6:12,14,15).

In the salvation experience, if we understand the grace of God and our sinful state for Christ — we then can forgive others. When I see people who refuse to forgive, I have to wonder if they understand the Gospel of Jesus. We have a weapon against Satan, it is called *unconditional forgiveness*. We sometimes have to make the first move to be peacemakers. We are to pursue peace. "Blessed are the peacemakers for they shall inherit the kingdom of God" (Matthew 5:9).

Ye have heard that it was said by them of old time, Thou shalt not kill; and whosoever shall kill shall be in danger of the judgment:

But I say unto you, *That whosoever is angry with his brother* without a cause shall be in danger of the judgment: and whosoever shall say to his brother, Raca, shall be in danger of the council: but whosoever shall say, Thou fool, shall be in danger of hell fire.

Therefore if thou bring thy gift to the altar, and there rememberest that thy brother hath ought against thee;

Leave there thy gift before the altar, and go thy way; first be reconciled to thy brother, and then come and offer thy gift.

Agree with thine adversary quickly, whiles thou art in the way with him; lest at any time the adversary deliver thee to the judge, and the judge deliver thee to the officer, and thou be cast into prison.

Matthew 5:21-25

A second characteristic of the spirit of reconciliation is the spirit of unity.

The quote comes from the Sermon on the Mount (Matthew 5:25). Jesus illustrated the severity of holding anger or bitter offense. If one is angry with his brother without cause, he is in danger of judgement. Jesus is exhorting us to *reconcile* even if the offense is not our fault. It takes maturity to walk in humility in order to bring *reconciliation*. But taking the first step is often harder for the one who is hurting. That's why Jesus told the person who caused the offense to "go to him." Paul in Romans said to "pursue and be a peacemaker" (Romans 14:19).

As we pursue peace — we must also pursue unity. We all have to start working together and not separately. STOP forming denominations and start *networking*. We have to stop running when we get offended, but humbly pursue peace and reconciliation. It will not just happen.

We have to pursue it. We have to pursue unity (John 3 17:11, Ephesians 4:3, 1 Corinthians 12).

We have to become one. We have to come to the *unity of the faith* and the corporate anointing will come into full power to perform the work that God has instilled upon us. It will not take the work of a few, but the entire body coming together in unison.

In Chicago, I am involved in putting on the "March for Jesus" event (North Shore). The purpose of the march is to show the world that *ALL* Christians can come together for one purpose only — *to celebrate Jesus.* When the world sees our unity; all denominations, all colors — then they will understand the power of God. The world is watching. Let us pursue unity, peace, and love. Let's break the power of division and walk in God's *power of reconciliation*.

Are you ready to walk in financial freedom? We must first cross the next hurdle, *the spirit of debt*.

Chapter 8
The Spirit of Debt

Now the LORD had said unto Abram, Get thee out of thy country, and from thy kindred, and from thy father's house, unto a land that I will shew thee:

And I will make of thee a great nation, and *I will bless thee,* and make thy name great; and *thou shalt be a blessing:*

And I will bless them that bless thee, and curse him that curseth thee: and in thee shall *all families of the earth be blessed.*

Genesis 12:1-3

What was God's agreement for Abram:

- I will make thee a great nation.
- I will bless thee.
- I will make thy name great.

I will say it as simple as I can, God's law of prosperity is, "You cannot be a blessing to anyone else if your finances are in a mess." America is up to their eye balls in debt. We spend more than any other country. Americans are declaring bankruptcy like it is going out of style. Unfortunately, Christians have fallen into the "trap" of the American way of life. Like most Americans, we need help in handling our finances. We need help in getting out of debt.

> But thou shalt remember the LORD thy God: for
> it is he that giveth thee *power to get wealth, that he*
> *may establish his covenant* which he sware unto thy
> fathers, as it is this day.
>
> Deuteronomy 8:18

Most Christians think this scripture says, "He has
given us the power to spend money. He has given us
the power to use our credit cards. He has given us the
power to buy anything we want." More than ever, we
need God's power to get out of DEBT.

I saved the best for last. As we end this book, we
will deal with the spirit of debt, the spirit of "the Devil,"
and the spirit of defeat. Any American football fan
knows that once you get within 20 yards of your opponent's goal line, it then becomes much harder to score.
In the same way, in these last three chapters, we enter
even closer to parts of Satan's kingdom that he has held
onto for generations upon generations. Satan will *not*
give up this territory very easily; in fact, it will be an all-
out fight. As we continue this book, we are going to
shed light on how Satan has blinded us in this key area
of *MONEY*.

> And Adam knew Eve his wife; and she conceived,
> and bare Cain, and said, I have gotten a man from the
> LORD.
>
> And she again bare his brother Abel. And Abel
> was a keeper of sheep, but Cain was a tiller of the
> ground.
>
> And in process of time it came to pass, that Cain
> brought of the fruit of the ground an offering unto the
> LORD.
>
> And Abel, he also brought of the firstlings of his
> flock and of the fat thereof. And the LORD had
> respect unto Abel and to his offering:

*But unto Cain and to his offering he had not respect.
And Cain was very wroth, and his countenance fell.*
Genesis 4:1-5

Abel gave a more acceptable offering than Cain. It should be no surprise that the *first murder happened over material things.* God rejected Cain's offering. So Cain killed Abel. We all know that God wants us to give 10 percent of our income to Him, but ever since Cain and Abel, there has been conflict and controversy in the area of finances.

- What is the *spirit of debt*?
- Why does Satan *fight* Christians so hard in the area of finances?
- What is God's *ultimate plan* for money in the last days?

What is the spirit of debt? According to Webster's Dictionary, debt is *"something owed to another"* or *"the condition of owing."* When I read this definition, I immediately thought of the word "bondage." You become a slave to the person you owe. There are many authors who discuss at length the subject of money. How to get out of debt, how to budget, how to invest, etc. Larry Burkett is probably the most recognized name in this area. Larry Burkett's principles of getting out of debt and staying debt-free are a must in our Christian walk. I want to stress the importance of *"getting your house in order"* as **Step One**.

(For if a man know not how to *rule his own house*, how shall he take care of the church of God?)
1 Timothy 3:5

Simply, how you handle your own personal affairs determines your success in ministry. How are you going to be used by God, if all your energy and time are used to pay your bills with the high interest rate attached to them? I have seen many Christians put on God's "bench" because they were out of balance in the area of finances. Our priorities have to be in order as in Matthew 6:37, "Seek First." Remember, money is not the problem; the love of money and mismanagement is the problem (1 Timothy 6:10). I call this *Step One* — "Getting your house in order."

But what then is *Step Two*? Why does Satan fight us individually and as a body in the area of finances? Satan knows that to do the end-time work of the Lord, it will not take millions of dollars, but billions. *Step Two* is taking our resources, time, energy, and finances — fulfilling the Great Commission. The everyday Christian has lost site of the *big picture*. Simply, the world is going to hell! We have miserably failed. We all know the scripture that says "money is a defense," but it's also a powerful offensive weapon (Ecclesiastes 7:12).

Recently my wife and I spent some time in Israel, as we were walking along the streets of Bethlehem, I asked Ascula (our tour guide), "where are all the Jewish people?" He told me the Muslims had taken over the city, I was shocked by the answer. The Muslim businessmen were buying all the property from the Jews. Whoever had control of the money, had the *POWER*.

We all know that God owns all things, all the wealth of the world is at his fingertips, but why doesn't God give it all to Christians? "If you are faithful in a little, God will give you much" (Matthew 25:21). God knows that most men and women do not understand the purpose of money and if God gave them any type of success, it would corrupt them.

Ye ask, and receive not, because ye ask amiss, that ye may consume it upon your lusts.
James 4:3

The devil knows the Bible, too. In the last days, there will be a transfer of wealth from the unjust, to the just. I believe God is raising up a group of people who will know how to handle the wealth and "*distribute*" it to finance God's end-time work around the world. The devil does not want to let go. I am not talking about individual wealth, but the Body of Christ putting their resources *together* to hit the devil with a mighty blow. What is the measure of success? When the job of reaching the world gets accomplished, only then can we stop. We are just too short sited.

Christians are basically selfish. We only give to local works of God; only a fraction of Christians tithe to their local church, and more people today have a poverty survival mentality, as opposed to an overcomer — *prosperity mentality*. Why should we strive to be prosperous? Very simply, to be a blessing to your own family and an overflowing blessing to others. *That is true prosperity.*

God is changing the way we view the pastor. Money is often a killer in the ministry world. When their ministries grow and the money starts to come in, they do not know how to handle it. They step out of the spirit and into the flesh, and that opens the door for the enemy to turn their blessings into curses. I will go a step further by saying in order for the modern church to be successful, we must run it like a Fortune 500 company. Most pastors think the anointing is all they need. As they preach on the spiritual blindness of the saints, pastors are blinded to running their churches administratively. Most pastors are good pastors, but terrible businessmen. Many pastors are good counselors, but bad leaders. Much like Daniel and Joseph, the position of pastor is going to change. God is starting to ask his leaders, "How have you used what you have?" Have you buried God's talents in the ground? The Bible calls one who does this a wicked, foolish servant. We have to change our survival mentality to an overcoming mentality to get ready for God's riches to come. More importantly, how to use these riches for the multiplication God wants to happen. God wants to prosper you (3 John 2).

What is God's ultimate plan in the End Times? God wants to possess the land spiritually and *economically.* With the blessing of God always comes increase. "It is God's desire to give you increase, which is the kingdom" (Deuteronomy 8:18, Proverbs 10:22). The purpose of the increase is to build God's kingdom, not your own (Ecclesiastes 10:19, Luke 6:38).

Spirit of Prosperity

And the LORD *shall make thee the head, and not the tail;* **and** *thou shalt be above only, and thou shalt not be beneath;* **if that thou hearken unto the commandments of the LORD thy God, which I command thee this day, to observe and to do them.**

Deuteronomy 28:13

It is time for the Body of Christ to assume their position as the *Head and not the Tail.* It is time for us to rise up and assume our rightful position of authority over our finances; in our families, cities, and nations. It is time for us to take dominion in this vital area — our FINANCES.

Poverty is a curse. The opposite of poverty is *prosperity.* How will be Body of Christ get back what is rightfully theirs? We have to not only handle our finances properly, but know the purpose of God's financial blessing. We must *DEMAND BACK WHAT THE DEVIL HAS STOLEN FROM US.* It is "PAYBACK DAY" for the Body of Christ.

> And David inquired at the LORD, saying, Shall I pursue after this troop? shall I overtake them? And he answered him, Pursue: for thou shalt surely overtake them, and without fail *recover all.*   1 Samuel 30:8

Like David, who lost his finances to the devil at Ziglag, it is time for the Body of Christ to *recover all* now. Not only are we fighting for us, but for our children as well — *our inheritance.* We have to do this by faith, as we realize our position of authority in Christ and realize that the devil has stolen our blessings from us. It is time to get mad at the devil, DEMANDING our blessing back. It is time to get ready for the transfer "from the unjust to the just." I do not know about you, but God is looking for people He can bless, trusting someone to finance His work called the Great Commission. Are you that person? Are you that church? Are you that leader? It is time for the Daniels and the Josephs of the world to rise to the top. It is time to FINANCE the Kingdom of God, letting the billions of dollars come to do the work of the Lord. It is time for the spirit of prosperity to dominate our lives and the spirit of debt to be cancelled. It is time for the Body of Christ once again to be the *HEAD AND NOT THE TAIL*.

Will you do your part in funding God's harvest (Deuteronomy 8:18)? God is looking for a new breed of saints who want more than just getting by. God is raising up saints with the God-given power to get wealth. Once they get it, that wealth will be put to use to *establish the covenant* of God throughout the earth. Those riches will be directed into the hands of Christian churches and God honoring ministries to use, to finance God's end-time global revival that is now ripe for the reaping.

The next step — you must pass through the devil, the spirit of "the devil".

Chapter 9
The Spirit of "The Devil"

The fear of the LORD is to hate evil: *pride, and arrogancy,* and the evil way, and the froward mouth, do I hate.

Proverbs 8:13

As we get closer to the goal-line, it gets tougher and tougher. Satan's forces dig in, they do not want to give up ground. One of the strongest forces that works against you, especially when you get close to the goal line, when you start to see growth in your church, when God is blessing your life, is the spirit of pride - I call it the spirit of "The Devil." God does not play with the spirit of pride. In His Word, He says, "He hates it."

What is the spirit of Pride? Another name the Bible uses for the spirit of pride is Leviathan. He is called both a dragon and a serpent. The scriptures describe him as a powerful, wily foe and a nightmarish monster usually described as a sea creature (Isaiah 27:1). What are some examples of the symptoms when you are operating in the spirit of pride? The things you used to do that got you where you are (back in God's graces), *you stop doing.* You are not spending as much time with God in prayer. You are not spending as much time in the Word. You are not spending as much time with other Saints. You are accountable to no one. You are not listening to advice from others. You have become unteachable. You think you are being submissive to God, but you are in full rebellion and you do not even know it. You are in major denial to your spiritual condition, others around you see it, but you are blind to your fallen condition. Instead of leading your army into battle, you now sit back and relax, your armor of defense is down. You think you are invincible, but little do you know, *that your doom is around the corner.*

> *Pride goeth before destruction,* **and an haughty spirit before a fall.**
>
> **Proverbs 16:18**

I believe ministers of the Gospel, especially those in the *five-fold ministry* have not yet dealt properly with the *spirit of pride*, also known as Leviathan. Job 41 says, "canst thou draw out Leviathan with a hook?" He is a powerful foe.

> **And it came to pass in an eveningtide, that David arose from off his bed, and walked upon the roof of the king's house: and from the roof he saw a woman washing herself; and the woman was very beautiful to look upon.**
>
> **And David sent and inquired after the woman. And one said, Is not this Bathsheba, the daughter of Eliam, the wife of Uriah the Hittite?**
>
> *And David sent messengers, and took her; and she came in unto him, and he lay with her;* **for she was purified from her uncleanness: and she returned unto her house.**
>
> **And the woman conceived, and sent and told David, and said, I am with child.**
>
> **2 Samuel 11:2-5**

When David committed adultery and then committed murder, he was on the top of the world, and God was blessing him. So what happened? Instead of David being in the battle leading his troops, he decided to stay home. Pride swallowed him up into thinking — *he had arrived*! He thought to himself, "I have fought long and hard, it is time to take a break, I deserve a vacation, look what I've done for God." Temptation got the best of him. David did not just fall, he fell hard! He was so blinded by the *spirit of pride* it took Nathan, the prophet, to reveal his sin to him. Pride is a spirit that can cause you to fall. The sad thing is, many ministers are walking in the spirit of pride and do not know they have it. The spirit of pride is a "blinding" spirit. What I mean is, "you do not know that you are operating in pride, when you are actually walking in the full blown manifestation of its ugliness."

This is a spirit that a lot of preachers are blinded to, and there are *four areas* that the spirit of pride can negatively affect your ministry with. The spirit of pride in these four ways can keep you from, *Crossing the Goal Line...Ten Yards at a Time.* *"First, with the spirit of pride also comes the spirit of rebellion."*

For rebellion is as the sin of witchcraft, and stubbornness is as iniquity and idolatry. Because thou hast rejected the word of the LORD, he hath also rejected thee from being king.

1 Samuel 15:23

Why did I call the spirit of pride — the spirit of "The Devil"? Satan was kicked out of heaven because he wanted to be worshiped like God, thus, he rebelled against God. Have you ever met a person whom you could not tell anything? They are walking in pride and rebellion. Pride will come in and say, "you are doing a wonderful job, look at what happens when people come to your meetings, look at what you have accomplished for God." If you accept those thoughts, the big "I" will start growing in you, and then the "I wills" will move you from pride to self-will leaving you primed for a big fall. You cannot cross the goal line unless you stay on the team. In basketball, I could not contribute to the team if I fouled out. In the same way, I cannot cross the goal line if my pride and rebellion fouled me out of God's team. Trust me when I say this, "If Satan and King David failed from the spirit of pride and rebellion in their lives, do you think you are immune from its influence?" *Secondly, pride insulates you from God and man.*

> The wicked, *through the pride of his countenance, will not seek after God:* God is not in all his thoughts.
>
> **Proverbs 13:10**

> Pride only breeds quarrels, but *wisdom is found in those who take advice.*
>
> **Proverbs 13:10 (NIV)**

Pride insulates you from God. You stop hearing His voice. Pride also insulates you from man. You stop heeding godly counsel. As a minister, I have read many books on church growth. All I read and heard about are the large churches that have made it. What about the thousands of churches that have *not*? Sharon and I have known many pastors who would fellowship with us, but over the years stopped associating with us or any other ministry. They became a "lone wolf," separated from the Body of Christ. This erroneous thinking all starts with pride, rebellion, and then their thoughts become, "we are the only church that hears from God, we do not need anybody else." Look at church history and see how occult churches were formed, examples: Jehovah Witness, Mormon, Islam, etc. One confused man started his own religion in his isolation. Pride disconnects you from the Body of Christ, *then you become a prime target for Satan.* One of the greatest needs for leaders today is an *accountability partner*. Simply, someone who can keep you going on the "straight and narrow" with God. Someone who can speak the "truth into your life in love." Someone you can have a *"covenant"* relationship with, *someone who really loves you.* When you have the proper "covering" (accountability partner) over your life and ministry, then you have a proper safety net to protect you from the spirit of pride and rebellion.

Thirdly, pride produces spiritual decay.

You can have *"tooth decay"* if you do not take care of your teeth. You can have *"spiritual decay"* if you do not take care of your spiritual life, by guarding yourself against the disease of **PRIDE**. Pride stunts your spiritual growth, because it says you have arrived and no longer need to work toward maturity. Remember this; with God there is no beginning and there is no end, so there will always be progression. You can detect the spirit of pride when you see someone lose their teachable spirit. You see the attitude change from a humble, teachable spirit to an attitude that says, "I've got it all together, I have arrived." Because it is progressive and subtle, I call it the *silent killer*. In your home, one concern now regarding safety, is the harm of carbon monoxide poisoning. Why is this such a deadly gas? Primarily, because it is colorless and odorless. As Christians, we get puffed up with knowledge (knowledge puffs up), we could die with the silent killer — pride — right there sitting in the church pew.

Fourthly, pride hardens your heart.

Circumcise therefore the foreskin of your heart, and *be no more stiffnecked*.
Deuteronomy 10:16

I like to put it this way, you become critical of everyone else. You are right and everyone else is wrong. Like rebellion, the *spirit of jealousy* is linked with the spirit of pride. Pride hardens your heart, and mind, you cannot think straight. Because your critical heart breeds jealousy, instead of encouraging your fellow pastor in your community, you start talking about him and verbally tearing him down. If you are not careful, jealousy will stop the anointing of God.

How do you overcome the spirit of pride? There are *three ways* that I think will help you avoid pride:

First, never forget where you came from. You will stay humble when you remember where you came from and where God has brought you. You did not bring yourself there — God brought you. The Bible talks about pressing towards the "High Calling" of God, always looking forward. But we should never forget where we have come from. It is only by the grace of God that we are where we are, let us give credit where credit is due, TO GOD!

Secondly, do not believe your own press reports. People will start "tooting your horn" when you move out in ministry, but do not believe it. Instead, believe God's report that you are a humble servant who is happy because you are obeying God. That is why everything is working right, you are "tooting" Jesus' horn. You are giving him all the Glory, not yourself.

Thirdly, stay close to God and make sure you give Him all the glory. I remember when I studied Kathryn Kulman's ministry, she always opened and closed her meetings with giving Glory to God. Like Katherine, we must make a conscious effort to always give Glory to God. It cannot be done subconsciously. We must make the effort. It is impossible to stay close to God and stay in pride. Staying close to God will keep you humble.

Staying close to God will protect you from the trap of Satan, falling prey to the spirit of pride.

> *Humble yourselves in the presence of the Lord,* **and He will exalt you.**
>
> **James 4:10 (NASB)**

The spirit of pride comes in many forms. Because it is a crafty and hidden spirit, we have to constantly be on guard against it. We are nothing without God, and we have to make the effort to remind ourselves of that. Do not let pride destroy your ministry, and keep you from *finishing your race.* Do not let the spirit of "The Devil" — the *spirit of pride* keep you from being promoted. Let us all put on the "mantle" of humbleness and discard the garment of "pride".

As we come to a close of this book as we *Cross the Goal Line...Ten Yards at a Time,* we have already discussed nine spirits that desire to keep us from fulfilling our destiny with God — *deceit, doubt, discouragement, diversion, distortion, disobedience, division, debt, and "the devil."* All of these spirits are very dangerous and have stopped many great men and women of God. But this last spirit is the most dangerous. Why? Simply, in the battle with the above nine, you are still moving forward with God. God can nudge you back on course as you move forward with God. However, with this last spirit "the spirit of defeat," you have STOPPED! You have finally given up on yourself and God. So, let us have victory and fulfill our "callings" in life. For you must cross all *TEN* hurdles to achieve your goal.

You must overcome this final hurdle, ***the spirit of defeat.***

Chapter 10

The Spirit of Defeat

Jesus saith unto them, My meat is to do the will of him that sent me, and *to finish his work.*

John 4:34

When it is all said and done, you do *not* receive a prize unless you *Cross the Goal Line.* In baseball, you do not score any runs with men left on base and three outs. As Christians, we *all* have a purpose on earth and our job is not to start the work of the Lord *but to finish it.* Remember, Satan's main goal is to steal, kill, and destroy. His main goal is to stop you in every endeavor of your life. He will not stop until you give up and *quit.* In the preceding chapters, we identified the top nine spirits that Satan uses against the saints of God to keep them from fulfilling their purpose in life — *Crossing the Goal Line... Ten Yards at a Time.*

Why is the spirit of defeat the hardest to defend against? Simply, in the prior nine spirits Satan uses against you — you are at least moving forward in the ministry. If you get off track, God can nudge you back on course for your life. Through reconciliation of your error and God's forgiveness, you can get back on track. It is easy to steer a ship when it is moving, but if a ship is standing still (stopped), you cannot direct it. It can get stuck.

141

As the truth of Christ is in me, no man shall *stop me* of this boasting in the regions of Achaia.

2 Corinthians 11:10

The *spirit of defeat* causes you to loose all hope in God and man — things that used to mean everything to you. In Webster's dictionary, the word defeat means, "*to win victory over; to bring to nothing, frustrate.*" I like what Webster says "*to bring to nothing.*" That says it all. Satan comes to steal, kill, and destroy. Satan wants to reduce you to nothing. In ministry, we have seen ministers *start* great, but in a few years we do *not* hear of them anymore. What happened? What caused something that started out so strong to not make it? What caused something with so much promise, to fizzle out like a cold camp fire? One of the reasons is the strong presence of *the spirit of defeat*. What are some of the ways that the *spirit of defeat* keeps us from reaching our godly goals in life? What are some of the ways that the *spirit of defeat* keeps us from, *Crossing Our Goal Line* in life?

The Spirit of Persecution

Yea, and all that will live godly in Christ Jesus *shall suffer persecution*.

2 Timothy 3:12

We do not have to deal with persecution like other parts of the world, but if you are living for the Lord, *you will be persecuted*. As in John Bevere's book, *The Bait of Satan,* he talks about the *spirit of offense* coming to the Body of Christ, well, persecution will come, too. It is not *if*, but *when*?

For I think that God hath set forth us the *apostles last*, as it were appointed to death: for we are made a spectacle unto the world, and to angels, and to men.

We are fools for Christ's sake, but ye are wise in Christ; we are weak, but ye are strong; ye are honourable, *but we are despised.*

Even unto this present hour we both hunger, and thirst, and are naked, and are buffeted, and have no certain dwellingplace;

And labour, working with our own hands: being reviled, we bless; being *persecuted, we suffer it:*

Being defamed, we intreat: we are made as the filth of the world, and are the offscouring of all things unto this day.

I write not these things to shame you, but as my beloved sons *I warn you.*

For though ye have ten thousand instructors in Christ, yet have ye not many fathers: for in Christ Jesus I have begotten you through the gospel.

Wherefore I beseech you, *be ye followers of me.*

1 Corinthians 4:9-16

Troubles will come, *but we don't have to give up or quit.* You are only defeated when you quit. How do you deal with persecution? In love, but knowing that it will pass. If you know in advance that persecution will happen, then you will be prepared for it when it does come.

Many are the afflictions of the righteous: but the LORD delivereth him out of them all.

Psalm 34:19

Part of being a Christian is dealing with persecution. *Instead of making us quit, it should make us stronger.* It should test our character. It should strengthen our foundation of knowing who we are in Christ. It should make us more like Christ. Many are the afflictions of God's people, but God promised that He would deliver us from each and every one, even persecution.

The Spirit of Ahab

And *Ahab the son of Omri did evil in the sight of the LORD above all that were before him.*

And it came to pass, as if it had been a light thing for him to walk in the sins of Jeroboam the son of Nebat, that *he took to wife Jezebel the daughter* of Ethbaal king of the Zidonians, and went and served Baal, and worshiped him.

And he reared up an altar for Baal in the house of Baal, which he had built in Samaria.

And Ahab made a grove; and Ahab did more to provoke the LORD God of Israel to anger than all the kings of Israel that were before him.

1 King 16:30-33

King Ahab was one of the most wicked kings of Israel. He not only married a pagan wife, Jezebel, and erected an idol to worship Baal, but King Ahab had an even *deeper root problem* that angered the Lord. He had a *spirit of passivity* — a spirit that would not take responsibility, or take initiative for his life. As we discussed earlier, the spirit of pride is dangerous to our lives, but the spirit of passivity is just as dangerous. If you are operating in the spirit of passivity, then everything you do will be like "pushing a wheel barrow up a hill." Simply, every project you do is a major fight. Nothing ever gets completed. *Many projects are started, but nothing is ever finished.* As ministers of the Gospel, we have to be aware of the spirit of Ahab, realizing that this spirit is an enemy to your success. We have to realize that the spirit of passivity is an enemy that will keep you from *Crossing the Goal Line...Ten Yards at a Time.*

Lack of Vision

Where there is no vision, the people perish: but he
that keepeth the law, happy is he.
Proverbs 29:18

I heard a pastor in California describe this lack of
vision as *"lack of purpose."* Most churches today have no
clear purpose or "plan of action." We have to ask the
hard questions. What are we here for? What is God's
plan for our life? What is your church's mission statement? We all need to know and hear the "plan" for our
life over and over again.

And the LORD answered me, and said, *Write the
vision, and make it plain* upon tables, that he may run
that readeth it.
Habakkuk 2:2

We not only need to know the vision, but we also
must keep it in "front of our eyes," so we will not get off
track and quit. If you are a church pastor, you must
keep the "vision" of your church in front of your congregation. If you have set "goals" for your life, you must
"write them down" and keep them in front of you. For
"lack and loss" of vision has shipwrecked many ministries and individual's lives.

Lack of Endurance

Let us not become weary in doing good, for at the
proper time we will reap a harvest *if we do not give up.*
Galatians 6:9 (NIV)

How many people will go to heaven and see what
blessings they missed by giving up just one day too early?
As I was watching the Superbowl this year, the game
was close, it was a fourth down play and the offensive
team was within the *five* yard line of the goal line. This
one play could mean the difference between worldwide

fame and honor, or the team that use to be. What if the quarterback did not give 100 percent effort in that one play? What if the running back took it easy? What if the offensive lineman decided to rest at that particular play? Many times in life, a single incident can decide your fate and change your entire life for good or bad. Young David did not *quit* when he killed Goliath. What if David hadn't killed Goliath? You may *never* have heard of David and later King David.

> **And every man that striveth for the mastery is temperate in all things. Now they do it to obtain a corruptible *crown*; but we an incorruptible.**
>
> **I therefore so run, not as uncertainly; so fight I, not as one that beateth the air:**
>
> **But I keep under my body, and bring it into subjection: lest that by any means, when I have preached to others, *I myself should be a castaway*.**
>
> **1 Corinthians 9:25-27**

You have to finish the race to get the prize. You have to walk in the winner's circle to get the gold medal. In our travels to the Middle East, I talked to a man who described the growth pattern of bamboo. He said: "it stays only a few feet high for years and then miraculously grows as much as one foot per day." In our desire to see our church grow, we want a consistent church growth, but much in the same way as the bamboo tree, your church might not grow as fast during a season. *Do not give up, the growth season might be right around the corner.* The winter season seems long and depressing, but *spring* will come!

A man's car broke down with a flat tire right in front of my house. He happened to be a clinical psychologist. As we waited for a tow truck to come, I asked him what the number one problem was in the mental health department of his hospital. He reported that depression was the primary illness that he deals with. I then asked him how he treats this problem. He said that he has to convince his patients that their STATE of loneliness will pass. You *will not* always feel this way. That this too shall pass. In life as we go through our peaks and valleys, we have to keep our eyes on Jesus, not the temporary set backs.

For the vision is yet for an appointed time, but at the end it shall speak, and not lie: though it tarry, *wait for it; because it will surely come, it will not tarry.*

Habakkuk 2:3

The *spirit of endurance* will be key to obtaining the "crown" in your life. For many will not endure to the end. Many will be deceived and taken off the course of their life. Many will quit and not *Cross the Goal Line.* What about you? Will you endure to the end? Will you quit, when your finish line is only inches away? It is time for the spirit of endurance to rise up in each one of us, as we press toward the mark, as we destroy the *spirit of defeat.*

Lack of Foundation

And are built upon the foundation of the apostles and prophets, **Jesus Christ himself being the chief corner stone.**

Ephesians 2:20

The size of a building depends upon the strength of its foundation. A church's growth is dependent upon how strong its foundation is. If the foundation is strong, then you will *produce* fruit, even in old age (Psalm 92:10). I want everyone not to be *retired* in God, but to be *re-fired* in God. Amen! It is important that you build the foundation and structure of your church right from the beginning. If not, your growth and ability to finish will be limited. If you are a church leader, let God take His time as He builds your ministry's foundation. Let God do His work. Be patient in this very important area, for if you rush this crucial period of your ministry, it can stunt your future growth. A rule I found to be true; "the longer it takes to build the foundation in your ministry, the larger the ministry will become." So take your time. Be patient. For lack of a strong foundation will surely mean defeat. Let's "finish the race" overcoming the *spirit of defeat* by having a foundation laid by God.

Are You Out of Balance?

And when he had sent them away, *he departed into a mountain to pray.*

Mark 6:46

Many of the things that got you to a certain level you must keep doing, and more, to grow. If you study Jesus' life, He would minister to the people, but He would always slip away to an *isolated location* and get charged up again. He prayed until He was filled back up. If you are empty then you have nothing to give.

But they that wait upon the LORD shall renew their strength; they shall mount up with wings as eagles; they shall run, and not be weary; and they shall walk, and not faint.

Isaiah 40:31

Those that wait on the Lord will be renewed like the eagle. Waiting on God will bring balance to our lives. God is still our strength. "Not by might, nor power, but my spirit says the Lord" (Zechariah 4:6). If you try to do the work of the Lord in the flesh versus the spirit, you will become burned-out and all of your leaders will be too. We have to remember what it took to get there — *keeping God first.* We must not let our business and ministry priorities get our lives out of balance. Remember, God first, family second, and then your ministry. We must keep balanced in our relationships (marriage, children, etc.) social activities, fun times, work, and ministries. Are you in or out of balance? Have you positioned your life to come against burn-out? Have you achieved success in all three areas; "body, mind, and spirit." Let us not be defeated by having any area of our life out of balance. Let us achieve true success by maintaining proper balance in our lives as we *Cross the Goal Line...Ten Yards at a Time.*

Pressing Forward

I press toward the mark for the prize of the high calling of God in Christ Jesus.

Philippians 3:14

You cannot progress if you don't get over your past failures. Victory means moving forward. I have seen countless ministers never move past a certain point primarily because they could not forget the past. Thank God, for His forgiveness. Sometimes God gets you into a situation that the only direction you can go is *forward*.

And the LORD said unto Moses, Wherefore criest thou unto me? speak unto the children of Israel, *that they go forward:*

But lift thou up thy rod, and stretch out thine hand over the sea, and divide it: and the children of Israel shall go on dry ground through the midst of the sea.

Exodus 14:15,16

Like Moses, it is time for the church to rise up, forgetting our past mistakes, and move forward with God. It might be the only direction you can go, *FORWARD*. Your faith needs to be renewed with the understanding that the past is not indicative of your future with God. It is time to take a step of faith, moving forward crossing your "Red Sea" into the "promised land." Remember, your miracle may never come to you until you take that step of faith, moving forward with God.

Nay, in all these things *we are more than conquerors* through him that loved us.

Romans 8:37

Are you more than a conqueror? Are you willing to finish the race? Are you ready to run to the finish line? It is time to loosen a spirit of endurance on each one of us, *for it does not matter how you start a race, but how you finish?* Whether you are walking through the *spirit of deceit, spirit of doubt, spirit of discouragement, spirit of diversion, spirit of distortion, spirit of disobedience, spirit of division, spirit of debt, spirit of "the devil," or the spirit of defeat*, the key to life is — *NEVER, NEVER, NEVER, NEVER, NEVER, NEVER, GIVE UP*, as you *Cross the Goal Line...Ten Yards at a Time.*

Let us not become weary in doing good, for at the proper time we will reap a harvest *if we do not give up.*

Galatians 6:9 (NIV)

Other publications by Marcus Hester
Confronting the King of the North
Finishing the Job: A New Look at an Old Command

Other publications
New Apostolic Church (Peter Wagner)
Moving Into The Apostolic (John Eckhardt)
Confronting The Queen Of Heaven (Peter Wagner)
Binding The Strong Man (N. Duncan-Williams)
Taking Our Cities For God (John Dawson)
Purpose Driven Church (Rick Warren)
Primary Purpose (Ted Haggard)
Final Quest (Rick Joyner)
The Harvest (Rick Joyner)
That None Should Perish (Ed Silvoso)
Redeeming The Land (Gwen Shaw)
Evangelism That Works (George Barna)
The Effective Fervent Prayer (Mary Alice Isleib)
Apostolic Strategies Affecting Nations (Jonathan David)
Becoming A Contagious Christian (Bill Hybel)
The Winning Attitude (John Maxwell)
They Smell Like Sheep (Dr. Lynn Anderson)
Possessing The Gates of the Enemy (Cindy Jacobs)
Apostles Prophets And The Coming Moves of God (Dr. Bill Hamon)

Coming Soon!
The Feet Generation (Marcus Hester)
Achieving True Success (Marcus Hester)

Audio Cassettes
The Secret Is In The Snow (4-Tape Series)
Ten Keys To Financial Freedom (6-Tape Series)
Don't Faint Before Your Harvest (Single Tape)
Are You Too Tired To Birth Your Miracle? (2-Tape Series)
The 11th Hour People (Single Tape)

To order books and tapes by
Marcus Hester
Or to make ministry contact
Please write or call:

Family Life International
P.O. Box 9121
Winnetka, IL 60093 USA
Telephone: (847) 267-9431
Fax: (847) 267-9432
E-mail: club1040@aol.com

Visit our website at:
www.familylifeintl.com